How to Plan and Build
Fireplaces

By the Editors of Sunset Books and Sunset Magazine

LANE PUBLISHING CO. • MENLO PARK, CALIFORNIA

Edited by John Gillespie

Design and illustrations: Ted Martine

Cover: Design by John Flack
        Photograph by Glenn Christiansen

Special consultants: Paul C. Johnson, Tom L. Wheeler
        Glen Crownover, Lee Parker

Editor, Sunset Books: David E. Clark

Eleventh Printing August 1978

Contents

Home is where the hearth is

When settlers came from mild tempered climates in western Europe, the hostile Yankee winters inspired them to build massive fireplaces and chimneys. Family life clustered closely around the great hearth for light, warmth, and food. The durable housewife toiled in the direct heat of the open fire, with an array of grills, spits, and cranes, amber-glowing pots, pans, and skillets.

Then along came the cast iron range to relieve the cook of her more hazardous tasks. Clearly superior to the fireplace in cooking efficiency and ease of use, the cast-iron range of the late 1700s pushed the fireplace out of the kitchen. The fireplace then took over heating the other rooms of the house, but not for long. Another development —the cast iron air-tight stove—more efficient than the fireplace as a heating device, could be installed in almost any room. And it didn't require a 5,000-pound masonry chimney.

Presently the central furnace was developed with the distribution of new fuels, coal, and later, oil. It appealed to our grandparents as superior to half a dozen stoves or to a dozen fireplaces. Many people observed that the fireplace had "seen its last days" and was only a wasteful luxury. Bleak years followed. Thousands of homes were built without a hearth or with only a bogus fireplace and plaster logs.

After a while, people discovered that warming up to a furnace outlet was something less than inspiring. They missed the amiable fireside. Fireplaces reappeared—"for supplementary heating," their owners explained. Fireplaces have been welcomed back into the kitchen to cheer up that active room and to take over some of the savory forms of cooking too subtle for our new precision ranges.

Today, the fireplace is a standard feature in the structural plan for most new homes. Conceived through the bold and artful use of line and material, it blends into the over-all plan so that it takes its rightful place in the center of things becoming the heart of the home.

In the living room, den, or bedroom, the fireside creates serenity for one, a mood for two, or encourages fellowship in a friendly gathering. During stormy weather we take heart from the flame's defiance of wind, snow, and rain. But, perhaps most of all in this electronic day, we value the fireplace for its stubborn refusal to yield to the push-button.

Indoor campsite has hearth high enough for buffet supper, seating for large groups, and elbow room for relaxation. Architects: Marquis & Stoller.

Unique transparent fireplace shows garden by day—and by night, if outdoor lights are on. With garden lights off, the heat-resistant glass back of fireplace becomes a mirror, reflecting the fire. Raised adobe hearth does double duty, can be used for seating or serving. Design by Cliff May.

Fireplace fundamentals

A fireplace has both practical and aesthetic qualities. Here are the fundamentals of good fireplace operation and attractive design: How it works ☐ Seven kinds of fireplaces ☐ Choosing the location for family and guests ☐ Designing your fireside for decorative balance, styling emphasis, color, pattern and texture ☐ Structural limitations and thermodynamics.

How it works

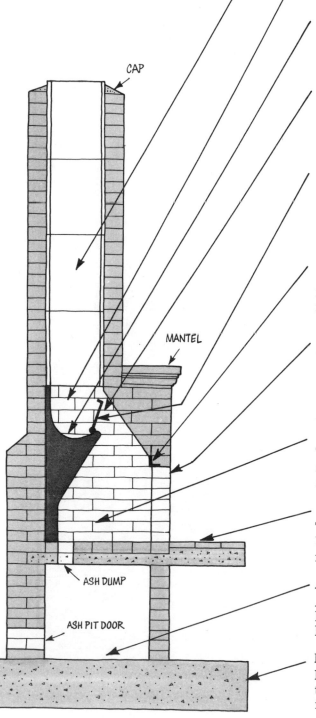

CAP

MANTEL

ASH DUMP

ASH PIT DOOR

Chimney Flue

Smoke and combustion gases from the burning wood pass up the chimney inside a flue. Flues usually are a large-diameter terra cotta pipe, or insulated steel.

Smoke Chamber

The smoke chamber acts as a funnel to compress the smoke and gases rising from the fire so they will squeeze into the chimney flue above.

Smoke Shelf

A smoke shelf bounces stray downdrafts back up the chimney before they can neutralize the updraft and blow smoke into the room.

Throat

The throat is a slot-like opening above the firebox, where flame, smoke, and combustion gases pass into the smoke chamber.

Damper

The damper is a steel or cast iron door that opens or closes the throat opening. Used to check and regulate draft, it prevents loss of heat up the chimney.

Lintel

The lintel is a heavy steel brace that supports the masonry above the fireplace opening. Sometimes it is incorporated in the damper assembly.

Face

The masonry surrounding the fireplace opening is known as the fireplace "face." It may be built of various materials: brick, stone, concrete, tile, wood, or it may be a manufactured unit or mantel.

Firebox

The chamber where the fire is built is made of steel or firebrick. Walls and back are slanted slightly to radiate heat into the room.

Hearth

The inner hearth of firebrick or steel holds the burning fuel; the outer hearth of non-combustible material protects the floor from heat and sparks.

Ash Pit

Ashes are dumped through an opening in the hearth into the fireproof storage compartment below. Many fireplaces today omit the ash pit.

Foundation

Masonry fireplace and chimney structures have their own foundations. The concentrated weight is usually carried by a reinforced concrete slab.

Planning the fireplace

Fireplaces are like old western movies. There are the "good guys" and the "bad buys." And, as in the movies, the hero is the fireplace with the fast draw. The "good guys" efficiently draw smoke up the chimney. The "bad guys" leave you choking in the living room. And planning your fireplace properly makes the difference.

The heat circulator—no foundation needed

SEVEN KINDS OF FIREPLACES

The masonry fireplace

The standard steel fireplace

The heat circulator—masonry foundation

The contemporary fireplace

The gas-fired fireplace

The electric fireplace

Masonry fireplaces and chimneys are traditional. They add a dimension of strength, durability, and beauty to the exterior of a home. Formerly, their efficiency depended chiefly upon the talents and experience of the mason who built them. Today, however, precise ratios have been worked out by engineers for fireplace construction. Metal fireplaces can now be used as a core and surrounded by masonry. Whether you intend to build your own fireplace, hire a mason to do it for you, or plan to consult an architect, you will find it useful to look into how one is assembled. (See *How to add-on a masonry fireplace* on page 68.) Try to locate a builder who is actually engaged in a fireplace project. It will help you to see one actually being built.

Prebuilt steel fireplaces come in a variety of conventional designs. They are moved in like an appliance. You can find one suitable for any room in your home and for any location within a room. Available in either regular or heat-circulator models, these well-designed units are at least as efficient as a masonry fireplace. The "zero clearance" units can be placed safely and directly on combustible flooring. No foundation is necessary.

To install one, you simply frame-in the firebox, cut a hole through the ceiling and roof, assemble the chimney sections, and install the rooftop housing. To achieve the fireside appearance you have in mind, you can then apply a veneer suited to your home's interior. The whole operation can be finished in a weekend or even in one day.

Beyond their light weight and ease of installation, factory built fireplaces are guaranteed not to smoke. They carry ICBO (International Conference of Building Officials) approval tags (among others), are listed with Underwriter's Laboratories, and have acquired general acceptance in local building codes. Fireboxes are lined on the back and floor with thick fire-resistant material. Two additional casings surround the unit. They also include a damper and a sliding steel firescreen.

Prefabricated freestanding metal fireplaces are the easiest to install of all wood burning fireplaces. You simply place the unit on some noncombustible material, extend the metal chimney through your roof, and seal the opening. The fireplace is then ready to heat almost any size room.

Because their price and size are smaller than conventional fireplaces, sometimes their heating efficiency is thought to be comparatively less. This is not so. Freestanding fireplaces radiate heat from all sides. Since they stand free in a central part of the room, there is little heat loss. Even parts of the chimney radiate heat. Moreover, they warm up faster than conventional fireplaces. And like built-in units they are guaranteed not to smoke.

Prototypes of the freestanding fireplace are still with us. A heritage from the old school rooms and the age of the general store, the Franklin stove efficiently and nostalgically fills the need for heat in many mountain cabins. Although not styled along the conventional lines of a fireplace, it burns coal, wood, or charcoal. The Franklin stove can be used as a fireplace by merely opening its doors. With the doors closed, the fire burns more slowly and will keep a room warm all night.

Simulated fireplaces, both gas-fired and electric models, serve an increasing number of apartment dwellers and mobile home owners. Having various BTU ratings, they can provide either primary or supplementary heat. They are available in attractive decorator colors and finishes. Recent improvements in design have made more than a few models convincingly realistic. Beyond their efficiency as heating units, gas and electric fireplaces have the advantage of being portable. You can take them with you when you move. Ease of installation is another plus. If you can hang a painting, you can install one of these.

CHOOSING THE LOCATION

Once you've decided on the kind of fireplace you want, a second question arises: *where are you going to put it?* The answer, of course, takes into account your family's way of living. Honestly examine your reasons for wanting a fireplace and see if you would use it more often in one location than in another. When the fireplace is new, you will probably use it frequently, regardless of its location. However, ask yourself where it will be most convenient to use once the novelty has worn off. Consider also the scope and kind of entertaining you do. For a properly functioning hearth, think about the thermodynamic needs of the fireplace itself. Smoky firesides result as often from poor location as from faulty construction methods.

Workshop fireplace *has subfloor hearth for easy after-work cleanup. Scrap can be swept directly into fire, large pieces stored for next fire.*

Your Family's Life Style

How will your family use the fireplace? Where do you spend most of your time? Does your family actually live in the living room, or in some other part of the house—the kitchen, for example? Wherever the family usually settles is generally a good spot for a fireplace. If you were forced to choose, would you select the living room over all the others?

Tradition dictates that fireplaces occupy the long wall of the living room. Contemporary interiors, however, have become so versatile that fireplaces are found tucked away into corners or installed at the ends of partitions, in the short wall, or even in the middle of the floor.

Alternate life styles suggest locations beyond the living room. Have you an artist in your family? A fashion designer? A talented handyman? A gourmet cook? The habits, hobbies, talents, and interests of individual family members help to narrow down the location.

In a spacious bedroom, for instance, sculpting, painting, sewing, or crafts often occupy cabinets and work areas. A fireplace here would have practical value when cleaning up after a work session, in addition to supplying the definite aesthetic of a bedroom fireplace. For a handyman's talent, a workshop fireplace can double in practical value. Not only does it help keep the place clean but also, properly located within the shop, it can serve rather economically as the sole source of workshop heat.

A gourmet cook is always part actor. The kitchen is center stage. If you have such an actor in your family, why not create something different with an early American kitchen-centered fireplace? Fairly compact kitchen fireplaces with adjoining ovens, cranes, and cast iron pots are available. Long handled utensils such as an imported Italian chestnut roasting pan and a French omelet pan are useful and versatile fireplace accessories.

A patio fireplace makes a comfortable outdoor setting for those cool evenings in spring and fall when you would otherwise remain indoors. The dining room, library, den, and family room are also areas to examine. Each of these is a possible site. Look carefully at your family's routines and interests to see if a hearth will fit your needs in one of these places.

A Friendly Circle for Guests

Remember that your fireplace will serve two groups—your family and your guests. How do you entertain? Formally or casually? Do you assemble guests in twos and fours or in larger

Southwest Indian influence *characterizes Tucson, Arizona, fireplace. Easygoing life style creates casual atmosphere among books, hobbies, and furniture. Architect: Arthur T. Brown, FAIA.*

Pool house rendezvous *serves guests in all seasons. Middle-of-the-room location allows wrap-around seating. Architects: Wertheim & Van der Ploeg.*

groups? Do you converse, dine, dance, play cards, watch televised golf matches or football games?

If you entertain even semi-formally, a fireplace in the living room would seem to be a necessity. But try to avoid placing the hearth where traffic patterns through the room must pass between furniture and fireplace. When family and friends are assembled, every to-and-fro movement disturbs the fireside group. Even a door viewed from the fireside is sometimes unconsciously disturbing; its presence threatens privacy and relaxation. The furniture should also be placed so that the firetender will not be forced to climb over guests, children, or pets when he brings in an armload of logs from the wood pile.

Remember this old maxim?

"No matter where I serve my guests
They seem to like my kitchen best"

If you want to keep your guests out from underfoot in your kitchen, make the living room hearth the most inviting and comfortable place in your home. Still, many a beleaguered hostess will confirm that, regardless of her best laid plans, guests seem to feel most at home in her kitchen. If this is true of your guests, you may as well join them.

The at-home feeling which surrounds a family room or kitchen hearth can create an ideal setting for casual entertainment. You can add a sense of drama to your informal get-togethers by using the fireplace to cook your party foods.

A guest room fireplace provides an accent of old-fashioned hospitality that will delight your overnight guests. Or imagine discovering a fire burning gently on the hearth in that ultimate refuge, the bathroom. No more cold tile floors on those chill mornings.

Fireplace cookery *in Spanish style kitchen becomes routine with special cooking tools placed for convenient use. Built-in fireplace is manufactured unit.*

Quick and easy fires *for the bathroom fireplace with gas-fired log lighter plus wall-to-wall raised hearth encourage relaxation. Fred Hummel design.*

DESIGNING YOUR FIRESIDE

Good design requires proportions that fit a fireplace to a room and to a location within a room. The fireplace styles shown on page 13 suggest a variety of possible installations. While you are examining the styles, consider these practical questions. Will the furniture you have *and the pieces you plan to acquire* group easily around the fire? Will the fire be just as enjoyable for ten guests as for two? Will there be room in front of the fire for an intimate family supper?

Decorative Balance

Many people prefer a fireplace that is an important feature of the room but not the dominant one. Some want a fireplace that is paired off with another center of attraction, such as a bank of bookshelves or the view from a picture window. Others like a fireplace that indisputably dominates the room through its massive size, striking design, or unusual material.

Perhaps you own a dominating piece of furniture like a grand piano, a stereo-television console, or a decorator's piece. To keep it from quarreling with the fireplace for the center of attention, you may have to plan for orienting the room toward both it and the hearth. Or you may decide to pull the opposition into the hearth's circle. You might need the conciliatory services of a decorator to solve this contest.

Styling Emphasis

Design of the fireplace facing can be worked out either to accentuate or to minimize the fireplace. The styles shown on page 13 may help you to visualize the emphasis of facing designs. If, for example, you want to blend your fireplace inconspicuously into the room, you can extend the mantel line to tie in other elements such as shelving, counters, cabinets, or windows. Or you can extend the hearth to join with steps, planter boxes, built-in benches, or couches. To dramatize your fireplace, you can shape its lines to contrast with those lines that mainly predominate in the room. Thus, the angular form of a hood will emphasize the fireplace in a boxy room, strong vertical mortar joints will appear to raise a low ceiling, strong horizontal lines to widen a narrow room.

Various structural devices can also be used to dramatize or to simplify the hearth. A cantilevered hearth is dramatic. For simplicity, a fireplace set into a wall or partition may seem merely a part of the wall. A massive application of

Single face fireplace

Freestanding fireplace, suspended hood

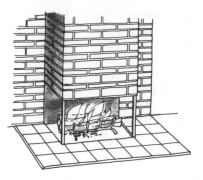

Three faces (2 short, 1 long)

L-shaped or Swedish hearth

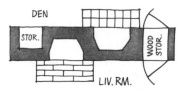

Fireplaces on opposite sides of wall

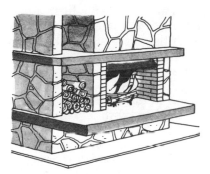

Cantilevered room divider

Raised hearth, projected mantel

Arched lintel (pueblo adobe style)

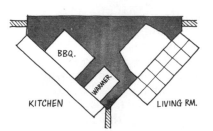

Multi-unit, combined foundation

Corner fireplace

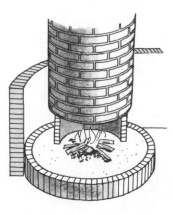

Semi open firepit (custom design)

Projected mantel

Combination unit

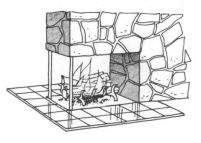

Three faces (2 long, 1 short)

masonry veneer will give the fireplace preeminence in the room. Tucked away in a corner, or angled across one, the hearth can suggest seclusion with eye-catching appeal. For ultimate impact, nothing can approach the freestanding fireplace placed alone in the middle of everything.

Color, Pattern, and Texture

These qualities of veneer materials depend mainly upon personal preference. No formula has been devised to guarantee proper decorative balance. However, you can usually rely on your own good judgment. Some helpful guidelines for selecting veneer are the room's walls, floor covering, cabinet work, and furnishings. An unobtrusive hearth, for instance, is achieved by covering it with the same material that blankets your walls. For a harmonious interior, consider the soft tones of brick and the warm hues of wood paneling. To create a dominating fireplace, rough concrete, dressed stone, or shining metal can be used in contrast with a bland interior.

The choice is wide. Materials with a long fireplace tradition are brick, fieldstone, adobe, tile, marble, and wood. For a less traditional approach, consider contemporary materials such as corrugated iron, plastic sheeting, artificial masonry applications, sculptured concrete, and finely etched copper.

Left, *panel wall, tile face, stone hearth.* **Right,** *raised hearth of fitted stone, conical steel hood.*

Structural Limitations

It may be necessary to use a single chimney to vent a furnace, kitchen range, barbecue, or additional fireplace located in the basement recreation room, a second floor bedroom, or on the patio. If you are planning a masonry fireplace, obviously such construction will restrict the choice of a chimney site. Remember also that location of the chimney may affect its drawing efficiency. (See page 88.)

Thermodynamics. Optimum dimensions have been worked out by heating engineers after a careful study of fireplace operations. There are, for example, serious differences in the amount of heat a fireplace provides, depending on whether you put the fireplace in the long wall or the short wall of a room. For the suggested width of fireplace opening appropriate to the size of your room, see page 65.

The heating action of a fireplace is principally that of radiation from the back wall, the sides, the hearth, and the fire itself. Because radiant heat travels in straight lines, its range is limited. The exception to this general rule is the heat-circulating fireplace, which heats by means of convection. Heat is distributed by air currents resulting from unequal temperatures and consequent unequal densities. A heat-circulating unit can maintain an even temperature throughout the room, whereas the conventional fireplace warms only that part of the room which is near the fire and in a direct line with the fireplace opening.

Left, *steel support post, steel plate and brick.* **Right,** *tile, brick, metal hood and paneling.*

The place of the fire

Although tradition suggests installing a fireplace in the living room, contemporary life styles ask greater versatility from our hearths. Today the fireplace is almost as portable as furniture. You can install one in any room in your home. In this section you can examine the rooms of your home one by one. Note that the photographs show several locations within each room for possible fireplace sites. From tradition's centrally located living room hearth to the engaging luxury of a bedroom fireside, the place of the fire is a place to enjoy.

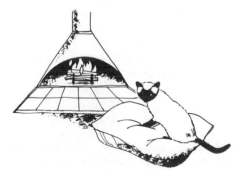

The whole wall is a fireplace

Focal point *in a spacious room: solid brick wall, ornamentation, flanking artifacts and books, lintel in alternate brick pattern. Mark Vorhis design.*

A wall of stone can be a benevolent monarch or a dominating tyrant in your living room. Its imperial attitude depends upon your furnishings and the room's general character. Draperies should cover walls and/or windows generously. Chairs, tables and sofas will have a timid look if they are not in proportion to the massive fireplace wall.

If not treated with sublety, such masonry wall facing materials as brick, aggregate, tile, slate and flat stone may have a monotonous or oppressive effect. Variations in pattern help; brickwork, for instance, can be laid in basket weave, or aggregate sections in an alternating pattern. With the great variety of tile shapes, styles and colors available, designing your fireplace wall could be a separate project all by itself. Slate needs the definite relief of a rough hewn plank or lintel-like mantel. Leave the mantelpiece unfinished on all sides except the top which you can polish and employ as a counter for serving family and guests by the fire. Oversized paintings or wall hangings have a multi-national look and relieve an otherwise monotonous wall. You can add to the richness of the room by leaving large open spaces between groups of furniture.

Or, try setting brass or bronze lamps into the wall. Another use of lamps is to install spotlights and focus them on the hearth.

(Continued on page 18)

Fire of long logs *takes fireplace out of the ordinary; a wall-to-wall fire is an arresting experience. Architect: Arthur T. Brown, FAIA.*

Rustic neighbors *enjoy informal get togethers in casual atmosphere. Field-stone surrounding brick fireplace extends to out-of-doors, blending fireside with rustic view. H. Douglas Byles design.*

Log storage balances fireplace built into brick wall. Noncombustible masonry floor acts as hearth in desert home near Tucson, Arizona. Architect: Arthur T. Brown, FAIA.

Fishing rods and frying pans, *fuel supply and fireplace add up to family fun. Raised brick shelf acts as utility for cooking. Design by Lutah Maria Riggs.*

Long cantilever *of hearth plus horizontal brick pattern contrast sharply with strong vertical lines of metal hood. Wall is divider of huge living room.*

The fireplace as room divider

When you build your fireplace, it is relatively easy to extend the construction on each side, thus creating a small wall. The depth of a fireplace requires a partition wide enough to allow for flanking storage areas. Use these as storage cabinets, bookshelves, bric-a-brac display shelves, a place for a portable television set, or an aquarium stand. Depending upon its height and location within a room, the partition can also provide privacy.

As evident from the samples that follow, a fireplace partition does not have to fill the floor to ceiling height. The open spaces in contemporary post-and-beam home designs have made this kind of partitioning almost a way of life .You can separate living room and entry hall, living room and dining room, or living room and kitchen-family room areas.

A counter-height fireplace, with ceramic or enameled steel flues, makes an arresting divider between living room and dining room. The dining room side can house glass front china cabinets and several drawers for linens and silverware. If the partition is between the living room and kitchen-family room area, each side can house a fireplace. Or, on the kitchen side you can have, in addition to the fireplace, a barbecue, warming oven, and a built-in recipe desk with a shelf for cookbooks and other homemaking tools.

(Continued on pages 20 and 21)

Fieldstone takes center stage between living and dining rooms. Inner hearth is below concrete cantilever to prevent smoke and ashes from blowing into room.

Fireside library with adequate light suggests leisure. Concrete block fireplace separates kitchen, dining and living rooms. Architects: Buff, Straub and Hensman.

Warmth and cheer *of used brick gives a colonial atmosphere to the home. Floor-to-rafter height of fireplace wall makes it appear part of house structure, ties rooms together. Francis A. Constable design.*

Ivy and painted concrete *trim this room divider made of sculptured stone. Raised hearth creates buffet or sitting space. Ample wood storage areas. Bassetti and Morse design.*

Darkened mortar joints *and warm brick tones blend harmoniously with tone and grain of wood floor. Raised, corbelled hearth accommodates wood storage.*

No cross draft here: *firebox is at right angle to windows. Tiles form top of concrete slab hearth. Brick wall is painted. Design by H. J. Williams.*

Fireside windows with a view

Pebbles, pillows, and Pacific Ocean *provide surfside fireside for serenity or socializing. Beach deck is at floor level of house. Design by Alan Liddle.*

A fireplace with a view helps to solve the decorating problem in a room with a window wall. Where the fireplace and the view are combined, furniture need not be arranged for two separate centers of interest. And floor to ceiling pull draperies permit closing out the view, thus altering the character of the room.

Unique is the glass backed fireplace. At night, when the outdoor lights are on, you can see the garden through the fire. When the lights are off, the glass reflects the fire like a mirror. Where such a fireplace is flanked by windows, sitting beside the fire is an arresting experience.

The secret is to design this fireplace so that the draft moves forward up the chimney, pulling the heat away from the glass at the back of the fireplace. Otherwise, you will need a very expensive piece of glass poured to exact specifications which can withstand very high temperatures.

In desert and mountain regions, a fire with a view can provide an evening's entertainment as you look out on rarely seen nocturnal wildlife.

(Continued on page 24)

On a clear day *or night, three prefabricated fireplaces command magnificent view from this hillside home. Architect: Goodwin Steinberg.*

Left, firebox construction is actually out of doors. Firebrick construction is channeled into metal flue. Cap and spark arrester are required in this wooded area. **Right,** view from indoor fireside is of lake by day, stars by night. Plenty of space for weekend guests.

Oriental outlook dominates high ceilinged entryway, dramatizes lower ceiling and occidental style of fireplace face. Asphalt tile floor extends airy feeling throughout room. Outside is Japanese garden.

Traditional companions, used brick and wood paneling create informal atmosphere for this country fireplace. Raised hearth and casual setting make fireside a natural gathering place. Wide open interior of rustic living room blends naturally with expansive view. Sim Bruce Richards design.

How to
light a
dark corner

A corner fireplace is an invitation to privacy. The cozy fireside in a secluded part of the room makes a natural setting. It can also have considerable dramatic impact, particularly if it is designed to angle across a corner and break up the rectangular shape of the room.

For entertaining, a corner hearth lends itself readily to conversation. The furniture is easily arranged in a friendly circle for better face-to-face contact. A raised or cantilevered hearth in a corner makes an ideal spot for serving an intimate family supper. It can become a buffet table where the fire helps keep the hot dishes from becoming cold.

A corner has advantages over a flat wall fireplace. Benches and couches placed against the wall fan out from the hearth. A semi-circle of chairs can be arranged. More people can be seated within the flames' circle of light and warmth.

(Continued on pages 26 and 27)

Two hundred years later, *Ben Franklin's practical genius adds warmth handsomely to corner of small room. Stove's heat shield and bricks protect wall.*

Quiet retreat *for solitude or conversation has raised, two-sided firebox. Bookshelves and desk at right (not shown) convert room to study when desired.*

Versatility of lighting, *near fireplace plus bookshelves at right (not shown) suggest room designed for reading and relaxing. Contemporary fireplace on stone.*

Old fashioned rustic corner *has heat-circulating fireplace. Vents at sides distribute smokeless heat. Mantel and supports are detachable portable units.*

Lava rock and coral chips *encased in teak paneling form the hearth for freestanding contemporary fireplace in recreation room setting.*

Handy wood storage out-of-doors for recreation room fireside. Color variety in used brick face, pattern changes add eye appeal.

Lounge area for informal entertaining; heat-resistant ceramic finish of prefabricated fireplace allows placement of free-standing unit close to combustible wood panel wall.

Roaring fire adds to definite dominance of brick walls and long hood. Fireplace draft from two directions makes large fire possible. Pavilion style sitting room seen from bedroom side; folding partition divides room. Glass wall at left is exit to patio.

The family dines by firelight

Architects have recognized that the typical American family often likes to gather in the kitchen. So they have designed kitchen-dining rooms that are comfortable and inviting — a friendly place in which to visit, eat, play cards, do homework, watch television and, incidentally, cook. Rare is the hostess who does not agree that "all good parties end in her kitchen." Guests, it seems, insist on feeling at home.

To create an atmosphere of warmth and overall good fellowship, designers have used warm-toned woods, amiable wallpapers, and—as a crowning asset — small raised fireplaces. Most kitchen fireplaces are equipped with such cooking devices as a barbecue grill or a pot crane.

Dinner beside the hearth can mean the dining room, family room, or kitchen, usually depending on where the food is prepared. If you want to do a greater variety of cooking in the fireplace itself, you might consider the swinging pole grills that adjust to fit your fireplace opening and several types of wrought iron hooks that are bolted to the inside of the fireplace. These can be found in stores specializing in fireplace accessories. The more expensive types of fireplace hooks have a bracket that is permanently bolted to the inside wall of the fireplace. The hook fits into this bracket and can be removed when not in use.

(Continued on page 30)

Dutch door passage *from kitchen creates a tall fireplace island next to dining area. Hanging plants, warm woods contrast with simplified modern decor.*

Couch at left *beyond counter helps create relaxed, at-home feeling around fireside focused on kitchen-family room. Wood paneling ties room together.*

Heat circulator *takes chill off food preparation. Long-handled cooking tools allow convenient fireplace cooking. Guests who like to gather in the kitchen find this one an adventure. Large pot fits into fireplace.*

New family room, *large fireplace are pleasantly open to garden, serve for parties or more intimate family use. Uncarpeted, pegged hardwood floor is used for dancing. Acoustical ceiling controls sound. Sliding glass doors open to generous sized redwood deck.*

Hilltop house fireside in Mill Valley, California, was designed to capture spectacular view. Fireplace has cantilevered hearth for sitting or serving, generous wood storage. Architects: Marquis & Stoller.

Two hundred years of cooking, heating and open fires testify to the Franklin stove's efficiency. This updated model came along in 1869.

Fire in the bedroom

A bedroom fireplace can be an engaging luxury or an open minded attempt to meet personal requirements. In a busy household, space and privacy are often scarce. The bedroom can be a temporary retreat or a regular working place with a desk, tables, and cabinets for sewing, crafts, painting, sculpting, reading, or writing. Almost any creative endeavor requires a bit of solitude.

For picturesque nostalgia, use a wood-burning stove. (See pages 90-95.) A freestanding fireplace gives a contemporary look. Each can provide more heat then you will ever need. They warm up fast and radiate heat from all sides, even from the chimney pipes. A conventional fireplace built into a corner makes a pleasant sitting room.

A bedroom fireplace can be economical if you spend much time there. With a bedroom fireside you can turn down the central furnace, warm up comfortably by the fire, and hold down your heating bill at the same time.

(Continued on pages 32 and 33)

Antiques and bare floors *fit comfortably with European peasant design of fireplace. Lower part is painted adobe, breast is of plaster. Fluted appearance was patted into shape by hand.*

Elegant brass ember guard and andirons decorate fireplace in room that is versatile by design—sitting room, sewing center, reading room, and, incidentally, a bedroom.

Warm and friendly *attic fireplace takes chill from frosty mornings. Face of fireplace is Arizona flagstone. Hearth at lower level uses same chimney.*

Western, Spanish and Indian *cultures blend with simple bedroom fireplace. Raised brick hearth and natural corner setting have practical uses.*

Reading, writing, and visiting *in comfort is the idea behind this bedroom fireplace. Chimney is also used for ground floor living room fireside. Metal hood has an insulated lining.*

The indoor-outdoor fireplace

Every kind of fireplace is at home out of doors. Probably no other part of your home offers a greater challenge than your outdoor living area. Location possibilities are numerous. The middle of the back lawn, a terrace, lanai, outdoor-indoor room adjacent to the house, deep porch, the border of a deck, or beside the pool. Trees furnish fine natural shelter, although low hanging branches can be damaged by the smoke and heat from an open fireplace. Perhaps you own a hillside lot that needs a retaining wall before you can build a recreation area.

Selecting the fireplace and barbecue equipment and accessories is a challenge also. Take an idea tour through the seemingly endless variety of outdoor fireplace and barbecue equipment and accessory marketplaces—garden supply centers, building supply houses, hardware stores, supermarkets, patio shops, department stores, fireplace specialty shops, and masonry supply yards. For a wider selection, ask these distributors for the names and addresses of manufacturers. Write for their illustrated brochures.

Having a professionally built outdoor fireplace setting that you can enjoy is a matter of

Patio pivot is performed by freestanding metal unit. Fireplace turns easily toward indoors or faces out to recreation area. Sliding doors close completely.

Bowl in the wall fireplace serves indoor and outdoor dining areas. Hood has metal damper to close off one side while other is in use. Stephen Oyakawa design.

Combination barbecue and fireplace *takes center stage in this airy outdoor room. Red brick unit has gas burner with wood storage beneath (at left); sink is at right.*

finding a reliable builder. If, however, you definitely want to build the installation yourself but lack of "how-to" knowledge has kept you from getting started, take your general ideas to an architect. In an hour or two, at surprisingly low cost, you can have an improved plan (plus a few ideas that you hadn't thought of) and will feel encouraged to begin. You can control costs by building your outdoor setting in sections. Work out the general plan, then put it together a little at a time. A large installation can be projected over several summers. By starting with some simple construction, you can use the fireplace area right away. Your enjoyment of the outdoor setting will then spark your enthusiasm and increase your fund of creative ideas about its expansion.

When planning your outdoor fireplace, here are a few things to keep in mind:

• Out in the free circulating air, fireplaces do not require the tall chimneys needed indoors. They can get by with short chimneys or none at all.

• If a fireplace and barbecue are built as separate units and are attached to the house, however, each requires a separate flue. The flues should be separately capped or have different heights to avoid downdrafts.

(Continued on page 36)

Patio dining room *has small fireplace built into rough plastered wall in corner. Flanking tiled steps for gardening in containers adds to attractiveness.*

Western size fireplace/barbecue *set in adobe wall has grate-level control, sliding metal doors, generous counter space, storage lockers for fuel and tools.*

• A barbecue and fireplace combined as a single unit should have only one flue — but the flue should be at least one size larger than necessary for an ordinary fireplace. Grease smoke is heavier than wood smoke, and barbecuing tends to create sudden puffs that need to be carried off.

• The flue should be still larger if you have a recessed firebed because the lowered firebox is shielded from the draft. It is wise to build a high smoke shelf to help prevent smoke from rolling back down into the firebox. In some cases a fan in the flue is desirable.

• Barbecuing frequently requires a multi-controlled damper, one that opens and closes by degrees. Open it wide at the beginning of your barbecue session. After the initial heavy smoke is carried off, the barbecue should be almost smokeless. Close down the damper to avoid losing heat.

For further ideas see the *Sunset* book, *Ideas for Building Barbecues.*

Sheltered by overhang *of cedar roof, sandstone fireplace is backed up by redwood exterior of house. Outdoor games and swimming pool equipment are stored to left of fireplace. Virgil Jorgenson design.*

Middle-of-the-room fireplace

For those who like their fires center stage, this modern adaptation of the primitive open fire dramatizes the hearth with ultimate impact. Yet among designers and builders, the freestanding fireplace is a subject of sharp disagreement. Some say that it is unpredictable.

A large fireplace opening of this kind requires a greater draft to keep the fire burning properly. But a fire is extremely sensitive to movements in the air—opening a nearby door or window, even walking past the fire too rapidly, may cause it to pull to one side and throw smoke into the room.

Therefore, the main problem is to supply enough draft to keep the freestanding fireplace from smoking and at the same time to prevent air currents from deflecting smoke into the room.

Some experts recommend that air be piped directly from outside the house to the fire. You can set a cold-air register, the kind used for air-circulating furnaces, beside the hearth and run a pipe under the floor directly through the side of the house. Or you can install the register in the firepit itself.

Another way to insure that combustion gases are carried off properly is to put in a fan. The best place for the fan is near the top of the flue.

(Continued on page 38)

Ready for anything, this center room brick circle is an entertainment center, barbecue area, indoor-outdoor facility, and daytime or nighttime place for just sitting and relaxing. Terrace doubles room size.

The Metal Hood

A metal hood has the advantage of needing no corner supports. If it is heavy, it may require substantial flashing, though, and plenty of roof support to prevent side sway. In addition, the metal hood is a good heat conductor.

It is wise to extend the rim of the hood well beyond the circumference of the firepit and to allow at least a 35-degree slope. Many builders advise a damper and smoke shelf or baffle in the flue. A flue cap can also help stop downdrafts.

Flue Area

Flue area should be about ⅛ the area of the fireplace opening. If anything, too much flue area is better than too little. Also, the higher flues have greater draft.

As with the conventional fireplace, the freestanding fireplace needs an outer hearth to catch falling sparks. A screen is also advisable. Check with your building inspector for local regulations. Also ask him about clearances. A metal firebox that isn't insulated can become excessively hot during the course of an evening. It is a good idea to place your firebox at least 3 feet away from walls, windows, and seating arrangements. If your draft comes from a window or door, anyone sitting in its path may feel the coldness of the blast. Conversely, an evening by the fire can result in some memorable burns, so arrange seating with this in mind.

Steel posts support fireplace

Hood with freestanding wall

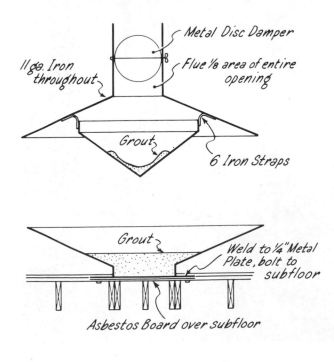

Insulated metal hood

Steel conical firepit

Rising twenty dramatic feet *from floor to roof peak, this fireplace has a central shaft 38 inches in diameter. Roof beams are 6 by 14 inches. Floors are of polished redwood burls set over concrete slab.*

Warm and glowing, *this prefabricated, hanging fireplace adds a festive touch to cabin living and provides a central gathering place; room doubles as sleeping quarters and living room.*

Every cabin needs a fireplace

The idea of a fireside in a mountain cabin brings visions of pleasant holidays to the imagination, evenings spent with congenial friends. Cabin dwellers confirm this fireside atmosphere, but quickly point out the necessity of a generous heat supply. Without adequate heat, nights in a cabin, especially a ski cabin, range from cold to frigid.

If you are planning to build a masonry fireplace and can get the whole family interested in hunting for fieldstone, the project itself can provide as much enjoyment as the finished fireplace. It will probably take quite a while to assemble enough stone for a good start on the fireplace and chimney. And, toward the end of the fieldstone search (especially if your children are helping you) the stone collection may tend to grow somewhat more slowly. Then there are the considerations of digging out for the foundation, mixing the concrete and mortar, and the specialized techniques of stone masonry itself. Nevertheless, masonry fireplaces give beauty and dimension to architecture and, when properly constructed, add permanent value to any home. (See "How to add-on a masonry fireplace" on page 68.)

A faster and easier way to build a comfortable cabin fireside is to install a prefabricated fireplace. Prefabs are ideal for cabins. The fireplace package (chimney sections included) can be put on a pickup truck or into a small trailer and hauled to a remote site for installation. Snap-together flue sections eliminate special tools, and simplified instructions help to make installation possible for the average cabin owner. (See "How to install a prefabricated fireplace" on page 79.)

(Continued on page 42)

Tent-like roof center *houses woodburning fireplace flue. Simple unmortared bricks in wood form serve as effective noncombustible cabin hearth.*

Chimney stack *of painted metal emphasizes living room's soaring space. Oak flooring was used as facing for the prefabricated fireplace; above it you see the master bedroom balcony.*

Through the firebox, *if you look closely, you can see part of small room which owners call "the cave." Game table is at far right; ladder leading to sleeping loft is also accessible from opposite side.*

Sole source of heat in cabin is the ceiling-suspended firehood. Hood radiates heat all the way up to high overhead. To right of hood is pulley-suspended kerosene lamp.

Hexagonal house and hearth were lowered to building site by rope from road above in remote area. Cabin has total privacy.

The face
of the fire

Accenting the face of the fire depends on the idea you want to express.
Here are eight ways to approach your design project. Choosing the
shape, color, pattern texture, and material can be a family affair.
You can cover a wall or build one, use masonry, wood, or metal for
your mantel. The possibilities are many; the chance to test your
creative powers, exciting.

Adobe adds the Western touch

Ever since the Spaniards brought the technique of making adobe bricks to the Southwest, over 175 years ago, these bricks have been used consistently for both construction and for finishing work. Western tradition has made them a natural choice for the at-home look in a ranch-style room.

Although made of a fairly durable material, adobe bricks are not noted for fire resistant qualities. Unless insulated with a hard-burned lining, they will eventually crumble away from the heat.

In modern homes, adobe brick fireplaces are most often found incorporated into an adobe wall, but occasionally the material is used only for a facing in combination with rustic paneling. Where the fireplace is part of a wall, the adobe is usually plastered and painted; where it stands alone, it is often left in its natural rich brown.

For an atmosphere that speaks distinctly of the West, of Spanish traditions, old missions, and haciendas, perhaps no material is more appropriate than adobe.

Adobe fireplace *and walls combine with open beam ceiling for Western contemporary appearance. Firebox border is painted firebrick. Extended mantel and hearth draw attention to fireplace.*

Fireplace directs *radiant heat throughout room from semicircular opening. Although very large, fireplace is proportionate to furnishings. Early Western ranch house living room shows Spanish influence.*

Wood walls are friendly

Gathering place *for guests centers around fireplace set in wood wall. Bold use of wood extends to bare floors, railings, outside terrace, general appearance.*

Consider the decorating choices. Paneling, board and batten, tongue and groove, laminated woods, parquet patterns, open beams and panels, covered plywood sheeting, or indoor shingles are a few of the ways to cover a wall. Add to these possibilities the variety of woods available—redwood, pine, oak, cedar, mahogany, or virtually any other available wood. Like a child in front of a candy counter, you may find that making a selection is a long term project.

Your furnishings can help to narrow the field. Is your furniture in period or contemporary style? Have you been considering the purchase of other pieces which will accent the present atmosphere of your room or give it a different character entirely? Look also at your walls, draperies, and floor coverings. The texture of wood may be used to harmonize or contrast with them. In a relatively nondescript room, a jolting contrast may be needed to liven things up.

The colors of wood and masonry complement each other. The coral tones of common brick surrounding your fireplace match the soft, warm browns of redwood and cedar. Buff colored face bricks blend well with the straw tones of mahogany or pine veneers. A marble firebox frame duplicates the watered-silk grain of birch plywood. Rough woodwork, like board and batten or knotty pine, provides an excellent casual background for a fireplace of dressed stone.

Stone bench *by fire covers wood storage. Wood wall paneling and custom chipped stone face combine harmoniously to promote warm, comfortable room.*

Old country style cottage fireplace has stairs (left of fireplace) leading around chimney to bedroom above. Paneling around fireplace is knotty pine, other paneling is red cedar. Two story living room has appearance and feeling of out-of-doors. Kitchen is at right.

Where books are a way of life

Scholarly serenity *beside a warm fire is created in conservative atmosphere of den. Pole lamp by reading chair suggests long, quiet hours of privacy.*

The presence of many books suggests a hearth that is frequently enjoyed. If books are a way of life in your home, the fireplace can carry the message of their importance very effectively. By positioning study areas near the fire within easy reach of bookshelves, the accent is unmistakable.

Books are perishable commodities, however, and unless you are willing to rotate them regularly, avoid placing the bookcases directly above the fireplace opening. Special books that are kept on a mantel should be set to one side and back against the wall. If your bookcases are recessed in the wall above a mantel, though, no harm will be done to them there.

Having the bookshelves in one wall with the fireplace at a right angle avoids competition for attention between books and hearth. If you have a corner hearth, you can construct shelves to the same height as the fireplace opening and extend them to the end of the wall. The top of the bookcase can then be used for a distinctively bound encyclopedia, frequently used references, or special handbound editions. You can set these off with house plants in brass or ceramic pots, sculpture, or other art objects.

Tall bookcases that flank the fireplace are definite attention grabbers. In this arrangement, both the fireplace and the books seem to be dominant without competing for that position.

Massive fireplace *of rough stone and large mortar joints dominates the scene. Leisure and study motivate furniture arrangement in oversized room.*

Colorful Mexican tiles *set into plaster create eye-catching frame for used brick hearth. Fireplace provides comfortable privacy in small den.*

Semiformal *fireplace setting dominates indoor-outdoor room seen from out-of-doors through floor to ceiling glass wall with sliding glass doors.*

Elephants and spinning wheels *blend with charm of traditional fireplace to create homespun atmosphere in comfortable ranch style living room.*

Simplicity itself—*a fireside, favorite books, comfort, and time to read. Conventional design of fireplace uses both firebrick and decorator brick.*

What height for the hearth?

High hearth *for sitting, serving or Santa Claus watching. Heat resistant glass back of firebox reflects flame. Simulated adobe surrounds firebox.*

Basically, a hearth is simply a rectangle of non-combustible material, required by building codes, that is laid in front of the fireplace opening to protect wooden flooring from sparks and runaway logs and to push the floor back far enough so that it will not be blistered or warped by the fire's heat.

With imaginative treatment, a hearth can do more than simply keep the house from catching fire. Floor level hearths may be spread over a large area to create a fireplace room-within-a-room or run along a wall to tie the fireplace veneer into the room's design or into an adjacent room. The hearth may be recessed below floor level to produce a fireplace sitting room.

A raised hearth brings the fireplace up to a more intimate height. This is a favored arrangement for small rooms, such as a den or study. It is also effective for a dining room, kitchen, or game room, where it is awkward for persons seated at a table to see and enjoy a fire burning at floor level.

Raised hearths may be built up solidly from the floor, either flush with the wall or extended into the room. Often such a hearth is designed with wings or extensions that can be used for work counters, benches, seats, or planting boxes.

Low hearth *is tile mosaic resting on non-combustible firepit floor below open firegrate. Metal hood, massive stone wall add to impact of this fireside.*

Almost a walk-in, *this massive, three-sided fireplace has welded steel frame support for flue housing. Stone foundation is extension of flanking stone wall. Airy feeling results from open window wall.*

Ideas For Facing **51**

Variations with mantels

In the days of the pioneers, when the fireplace was depended upon to cook the family's meals, the mantel was one of its working parts, a shelf for pots, seasonings, and hot dishes. Later, when the cast iron stove pushed the fireplace out of the kitchen, the mantel assumed a more formal air in the living room, becoming a resting place for the family clock, art objects, and candelabra.

A mantel can serve as a decorative unit surrounding the fireplace opening, or it can be a single piece of wood, metal, or stone cantilevered from the facing above the fireplace. You can extend the mantel along a wall or tie it into the top shelf of a bookcase. The material and shape of the mantel itself may be used as a device to bring together the fireplace veneer and the surrounding wall surface.

Handcrafted mantels are starting to reappear —such classic styles as the massive carved stone of the Elizabethan period and the architecturally precise mantels of the Georgian era. The elegantly decorative designs of the French Louis', which carried their influence into Regency mantels, and American Colonial fireplace mantels, which adapted old world styles in either simple or sophisticated designs, are both popular choices.

As the photographs illustrate, mantels can indeed be very different.

Unique mantel design *is repeated in wood hearth trim. Mantel is supported by cast concrete pillars.*

Resting on Roman brick *is concrete lintel surrounded by intricately carved mantel. Traditional andirons and ember guard echo brass candlesticks on mantel.*

Long wood mantel, *accentuated by brass accessories, fireplace fender, and early American artifacts, complement knotted cedar open beam ceiling. Design by Ulysses Floy Rible.*

Left. *French Louis mantel accents shell motif, fine scroll work.*

Right. *Another Louis has stately contoured pillars, is elegantly decorative.*

Left. *Georgian mantel of the 1700's demonstrates architectural authenticity.*

Right. *Italian baroque designs feature graceful Renaissance-inspired figures.*

The tall ones

Just as words are arranged in a sentence according to the meaning you want to stress, so does accenting your fireplace depend upon the idea you want to convey. Here—among the tall ones—the idea is dramatic impact. Unlike the days of the bland, predictable parlor, where the family clock graced the mantelpiece or grandfather's portrait looked down upon the scene, contemporary fireplace design more frequently accents the fireplace itself.

The tall fireplace suggests long, uncluttered lines. A buffet, sofa, coffee table, or long narrow furniture, arranged at right angles, tends to bow to the hearth's dominant influence. There is little room for argument with these tall fellows. Even a grand piano is subdued and drawn into the hearth's circle.

A room with a two-story ceiling provides an opportunity for facing the flue area of your fireplace with a single, room-dominating material. Depending upon your architectural layout, the two story room can also provide another fireplace at a higher level (see photo page 57). Because of the special construction requirements for flues as tall as these, it would be wise to talk with your fireplace building inspector about your plans. If you are thinking about building one of these tall fireplaces, the inspector will probably recommend that you consult an architect. All of the fireplaces shown were designed by architects or fireplace engineers.

Friendly blend *of brick and wood become even more companionable when mortar joints are subdued. Flanking panel-like cabinets extend warmth.*

Like a vigilant sentry, *this tall fellow stands guard over family room, divides entryway-reception parlor and upper level family living and recreation area.*

All the way up *to ceiling above second floor stretches this white metal prefabricated chimney. Ski cabin near Salt Lake City, Utah winter resort area.*

Ideas For Facing   **55**

Hoods
are handsome
and functional

A metal hood provides a dramatic and efficient feature for a modern fireplace. It can serve more than strictly decorative ends: it can also increase the effectiveness of the fireplace by radiating heat when it is warmed up and the heat of the metal encourages greater air circulation up the flue.

The lustre of the bright metal enhances a room that takes its tone from the natural texture, color, and grain of the materials built into it. A hood may be fashioned of copper, polished bright, left a warm flame red, or oxidized green. It may be made of sheet metal with antique finish, a white metal such as aluminum or stainless steel, or steel plate, finished a charcoal black to contrast with red brickwork. Texture or pattern may be added by sandblasting, hammering, polishing, etching, or tool marking.

A hooded fireplace can be simpler to build than a masonry type because it sometimes permits elimination of heavy chimney work and foundation masonry. Some localities permit a simple brick hearth and firewall, adequate for a hooded outlet, to be built right over the flooring. Metal hoods and flues call for the skilled hand of a master metalworker.

Grate full of logs *sits on ready, gas-fired log lighter buried in white sand. Steel rods, anchored to ceiling, hold low hanging hood in place.*

Culinary corner *for subtler cooking adventures usually brings gathering of family or guests to kitchen. Architect: Ratcliff, Slama, Cadwalader.*

Sculptured copper hood *radiates heat and serves as attractive cover for brick and concrete fireplace. Flue extends from ceiling to within few inches of base of hood. Inside of hood is lined with asbestos sheeting. Hood is custom designed and fitted over chimney. Design by Pietro Belluschi.*

Two-brick thick *wall holds scored copper hood over firebox. Hood has galvanized inner flue with 1-inch air space separation. Hearth is gas-fired from side.*

Corner fireplace *has simple black curved hood welded at seam. Flue extends through low overhang to roof. Hearth is ceramic tile; walls are painted adobe.*

These fires have many faces

A favorite contemporary setting is the fireplace open on three sides. The projecting corner fireplace at the end of a divider wall is typical. Another multiple opening fireplace is the see-through design. A standard fireplace is installed — but the back wall is left out. The back thus becomes a second fireplace serving another room.

But with these fireplaces go special engineering problems. They offer less protection from cross-drafts in the room and require more generous flues and dampers. A specially engineered smoke dome, available in seven sizes, is manufactured to handle this kind of installation. The dome has separate open and close damper regulators that hold the damper in position.

Flue size. As with the conventional fireplace, flue size depends upon the area of the fireplace opening. You must measure the *total* area of all faces. The minimum area necessary for your flue will be 1/12 of the fireplace opening area if you have a round flue, 1/10 if you have a rectangular one, and 1/8 if your flue is unlined. Some experts recommend making the flue area one size larger than minimum.

Damper. Because more air enters your fireplace, you may also need a larger damper to accommodate the greater volume of combustion gases. With a three-sided fireplace, it is wise to set the

Back-to-back fireplaces lead to economies in construction. You can use the same chimney for both flues or simply eliminate the back wall of a fireplace and let one fireplace serve two rooms. Or you can widen the view of the fire by opening the fireplace on three sides.

Your choice of location for the living room fireplace may depend on whether you want the extra fireplace in the dining room, kitchen, study, bedroom, or outdoors. There are several practical ways for laying out a back-to-back combination. Here is one way:

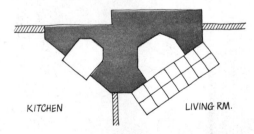

Another successful method arranges the fireplaces along a straight line with the wood storage cabinet set at one end and available from both sides:

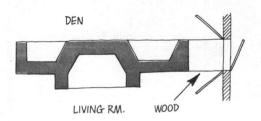

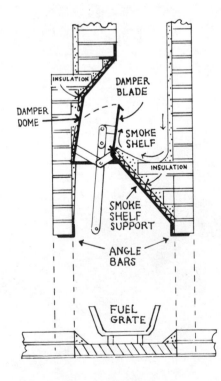

High dampers *and smoke domes are manufactured expressly for see-through and other multiple opening fireplaces. Cross section shows typical installation.*

smoke chamber back, so that it is not directly above the damper; otherwise, you run the risk of a downdraft blowing smoke into the room.

Drafts. Air currents are tricky, so before you put in a multi-faced fireplace, you may wish to consult an architect or fireplace designer. But some pointers may be helpful.

The slightest turbulence in the air may cause the fire to pull to one side and discharge smoke into the room. In general, it is safest to install the fireplace where its openings are not in the paths between doors and windows.

Lowering the firepit below the level of the opening will help prevent ashes from blowing into the room. Some builders recommend a fan in the flue to insure proper air flow up the chimney; but with a fan, you won't get much benefit from the fire's heat.

(Continued on page 60)

Frank Lloyd Wright concept: *stones are set in place individually as the fireplace is handpoured. Fireplace construction harmonizes with rustic design.*

Both living room and bedroom *fireplaces (see photo top right) have raised concrete slab hearth extensions and are open on two sides of firebox.*

Cooking tools in concrete *(charcoal bed, cooking grill and clean-out drawer); when concrete was poured, space was allowed for inserting kitchen equipment.*

Action center of room whenever guests arrive is this three-sided room divider, fireplace. Double flue is of terra cotta pipe. Wall is solid adobe; floor is of ceramic tile. Western ranch house architecture.

Braced against solid brick wall is three-sided hearth having same brick facing as wall; frame is painted steel. Long wide hearth of firebrick laid in weave pattern protects wall-to-wall carpeting.

Building the fireplace

The masonry fireplace: materials you will need □ building code requirements □ rules □ craft □ practices □ ratio charts □ step-by-step guide to adding on a masonry fireplace.

The prefabricated fireplace: what to look for when you buy □ building code requirements before installation □ how a heat circulating unit operates □ differences between freestanding and built-in fireplaces □ which chimney to use □ about gas fired and electric fireplaces □ how to install a prefabricated fireplace, step by step.

A new face for the old hearth

The way it was, *this attractive living room fireplace had little opportunity for aesthetic expression.*

The nicest thing you can do for a fireplace with an ugly mantel is rip out the mantel and replace it with something appealing to the eye. No one likes to sit and look at unpleasantness.

The Easy Way

If the weary appearance of your fireside discourages you from using it, there are a number of rather easy ways of revitalizing the hearth. Today's instant wall finishes make the project a simple one which rarely takes more than a weekend to complete. A whole gallery of classic mantelpieces, ranging from the Elizabethan period to American Colonial, are available. Wood paneling is less expensive, and even more economical are simulated bricks and fieldstone that are indistinguishable from the real thing. Simplified do-it-yourself packages are available from building supply houses, or you can hire a carpenter or mason to do the job. Also available are ready made hearths and fireplace surround units made of non-combustible materials.

A More Challenging Method

If you like to do things the hard way, you can chip off the facing and build a new one from masonry. As usually happens in such projects, though, the renovation project takes over the entire room, including cupboards, bookcases, and wall colors. A room with a tired looking fireplace is frequently a decorator's nightmare, its main

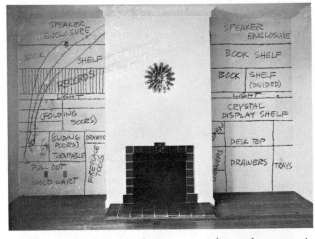

Some environmental therapy *is planned, room is stripped of furniture, wall measured and marked.*

The sound of music, *along with desk, and storage, contribute to character of formerly nondescript room.*

wall cut up with small windows or misplaced doors. Remodeling, therefore, calls for doing the whole room over, possibly relocating a wall or even the fireplace itself. Provided the chimney variance doesn't exceed 30 degrees, you can move the fireplace to the left or right by installing a "zero clearance" prefabricated fireplace, channeling it into the present flue.

For a really tough assignment, you can try tearing out the firebox and rebuilding the whole works. If the fireplace works properly and its unpleasantness is only on the surface, don't touch the inner parts. If an old damper must be replaced, however, such work is sometimes unavoidable. If you are adding a heat-circulator, which is guaranteed to work, tampering with the firebox in order to tear it out will not affect the efficiency of your new fireplace. But this is a mean, hazardous, and dirty job that is best left to a master mason— if he'll take it on.

A new hearth for an old place

Simple extension *of gas pipe through wall accommodates unusually tall, gas-fired fireplace. Unit hangs on ordinary wall hook, is thermostatically controlled.*

A warmer circle *is brought to this step-down living room area by adding a chain-hung fireplace. Noncombustible inlaid stone floor acts as hearth.*

The masonry fireplace

Masonry fireplaces are made of brick and stone, mortar and many man-hours. Painstaking efforts, patience, preparation usually produce beautiful result.

Masonry fireplace construction is hemmed in by a host of rules, formulas, and craft practices. Here are the basic requirements:

Foundation

The foundation that supports a masonry fireplace and chimney should extend into the soil at least 12 inches. In cold climates, the bottom of the foundation should be set below the frost line.

Reinforced concrete or solid masonry foundations will sustain the weight of a chimney and fireplace without sagging. The concrete slab should be strengthened with a grid of ½-inch reinforcing bars, placed 12 inches apart, and set at least 3 inches above the bottom of the slab. Foundations should exceed the chimney's width by 6 to 12 inches all around. Fireplace and chimney should never be supported by wooden floors, beams, or posts, because in time they will shrink or bend under the load and fracture the masonry.

Mortar

Rather than make two mortar mixes—one for the firebox and another for the rest of the construction—masons prefer to use firebrick mortar for the entire project. Here are recommended pro-portions: 9 parts mortar sand, 3 parts portland cement, 1 part fireclay. Add enough water to produce a fairly stiff consistency. In the firebox, slightly thinner joints are suggested.

Ash Pit

The ash dump and pit are conveniences to con-sider if construction permits their installation. They should be protected, though, from water, for if the ash load becomes water-soaked, it will permeate the house with disagreeable ashy odor.

Cover the opening to the dump with cast iron plate (about 5 by 8 inches), pivoted or hinged to allow ashes to drop into the pit below. Select a type that will not drop accidentally into the pit when opened. The dump cover is usually placed near the center of the back hearth, but it can be located anywhere in the back hearth if desired.

To promote easy ash removal, raise the sill of the cleanout door approximately 10 inches above grade or the basement floor for placement of ash receptacle and cover the bottom with mortar sloped toward the door.

For a fireplace on a second floor directly above the living room hearth, it is necessary to route the ash chute around the fireplace below. The change of direction should not be greater than 6 degrees to avoid ash retardation. Many second story fireplaces are built without an ash dump.

Facing

For safety, the nearest edge of combustible trim, paneling, or facing should be at least 8 inches from the sides of the fireplace opening and at least 12 inches above the top of the opening. But check your local building code for possible variances. Maintain a minimum clearance of 2 inches between all wood framing members and the fireplace or chimney masonry. Make the front hearth at least 8 to 12 inches wider on each side than the fireplace opening.

Fireplace Dimensions

To assure proper heating and to prevent the fireplace from smoking, follow closely the dimensions for fireplaces given in the charts on this page and in the chart on page 66. Too much variation will cause a fireplace to smoke and diminish the amount of heat it supplies. These charts were developed by engineers experienced in fireplace and chimney design.

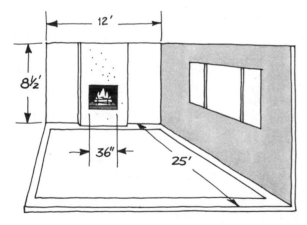

GOOD PROPORTIONS (RAISED FIREPLACE)

Fireplace Dimensions (In inches)	
Width	24 to 84
Height	2/3 to 3/4 width
Depth	1/2 to 2/3 height
Flue Effective Area	1/8 width x height—Unlined flue 1/10 width x height—Rectang. lining 1/12 width x height—Round lining
Throat Area	1/4 to 1/2 larger than flue area
Throat Width	3" minimum to 4½" maximum

Firebox

Back hearth and reflecting walls should be of soapstone or firebrick, 4 inches thick, or hard-burned tile, 3 inches thick. This thickness includes the fireclay mortar holding the hearth or wall in place.

To lessen the danger of bricks loosening or falling out, lay firebrick flat. On edge, they are only 2 inches thick and should be held in place by metal ties bonded into the main masonry walls.

If you build the back wall in the shape of a vertical curve sloping into the fireplace, not only rising currents of warm air but also smoke will flow into the room. To avoid a smoky fireplace, slope the profile of the back wall up in straight planes above the level of the lintel to the edge of the throat.

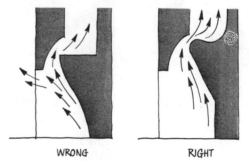

WRONG   RIGHT

Lintel

The minimum lintel required to support the masonry above the front of a moderately wide fireplace opening is an angle iron 3½ by 3½ by ¼ inches, enough longer than the opening to give a 3 or 4 inch seat on the masonry. For heavy masonry and wide openings, the size and thickness of these steel lintels increase in proportion. Provision should be made for expansion by wrapping the ends with fiberglass wool or providing some means for the steel lintel to move when heated.

You can build a masonry arch successfully if, at the sides of the opening, the masonry is

Suggested Width of Fireplace Openings appropriate to size of a room		
Size of Room In Feet	Width of Fireplace Opening in Inches	
	If in Short Wall	If in Long Wall
10 x 14	24	24 to 32
12 x 16	28 to 36	32 to 36
12 x 20	32 to 36	36 to 40
12 x 24	32 to 36	36 to 48
14 x 28	32 to 40	40 to 48
16 x 30	36 to 40	48 to 60
20 x 36	40 to 48	48 to 72

sufficiently reinforced to resist the thrust of the arch. The minimum thickness of masonry in front of the lintel or forming the masonry arch should be at least 4 to 6 inches and preferably more to avoid possible sagging.

Damper

There are many forms of dampers, usually combined with a metal throat. Some operate with a push-and-pull handle, some with a poker, others with a twist handle. A manufactured smoke dome contains a damper with "open" and "close" chain controls that hold the damper in any desired position. You can be sure of good results with

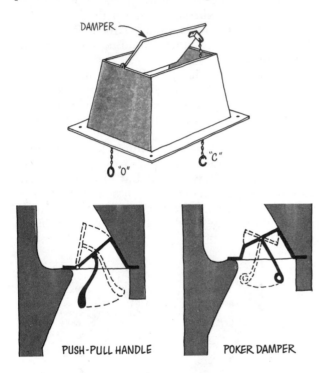

any type that is installed according to the manufacturer's instructions. Dampers should be set loosely in place and the ends wrapped in fiberglass wool to allow for expansion.

Throat

The throat, or damper opening, should extend the full width of the fireplace opening and have an area not less than that of the flue. Up to the throat, the sides of the fireplace should be vertical; about 5 inches above the throat, the sides should start drawing into the flue. The bottom edge of the throat should be 6 to 8 inches or more above the bottom of the lintel. The throat can be formed in masonry. To save time and labor, you can install a metal prefabricated throat or smoke dome.

Smoke Shelf

The smoke shelf should run the full length of the throat and be 6 to 12 inches or more front to back, depending on the depth of the fireplace. It should be given a smooth, concave surface.

Smoke Chamber

The smoke chamber extends between the side walls from the top of the throat to the bottom of the flue. Slope the side walls at a 60 degree angle from the horizontal and smoothly plaster with cement mortar or an equally smooth interior surface so as not to diminish the draft action.

Flues

Round flues are considered the most efficient for draft and smoke removal because draft-smoke columns ascend in round spirals. Corners of square or rectangular flues are ineffective areas, contributing little to proper working of a flue. Square or oblong flues are frequently used, though, because they are easier to set in place.

Multiple Flues. Each fireplace requires a separate flue, but you can locate two or more flues in one chimney. Separate them with a 4-inch brick or concrete divider wall, known as a "wythe."

Size. The capacity of the flue must match that of the fireplace. The chart below recommends flue sizes for sea-level installation (see the paragraph "Height of Chimney" for information on effect of altitude).

All authorities recommend that flues be lined with a smooth fireclay tile at least ⅝-inch thick.

	Recommended Flue Sizes (In inches)				
	Rectangular Flues			Equivalent Round	
Fireplace Width	Outside Dimension	Inside Dimension	Effective Area Sq. In.	Inside Diameter	Effective Area Sq. In.
24	8½x 8½	7½x 7½	41	8	50.3
30 to 34	8½x13	7 x11½	70	10	78.5
36 to 44	13 x13	11½x11½	99	12	113.0
46 to 56	13 x18	11½x16½	156	15	176.7
58 to 68	18 x18	15¾x15¾	195	18	254.4
70 to 84	20 x24	17 x21	278	22	380.13
Over 84	SIZES PROPORTIONATELY LARGER				

Although a fireplace should not be used as an incinerator for miscellaneous trash (which creates considerable soot), most people do burn trash in them. The fireclay lining will keep chimney residue at a minimum.

There are several advantages in using it. Lining reduces friction between draft column and masonry and lessens the amount of inflammable soot and creosote that cling to the inside of the flue. Lining also helps prevent cracking of masonry and mortar joints as the chimney expands or contracts during alternate heating and cooling. Without lining, the mortar and brick exposed to hot flue gases will gradually disintegrate.

Don't accept a mortar substitute for the lining. Chimney movement due to wind and temperature changes may cause mortar to crack and fall. This results in partial stoppage with consequent loss of draft and increased fire hazard.

Flues have better draft if built as close to a vertical line as possible. When a change in direction is necessary, it should not exceed 30 degrees from vertical nor should it reduce the flue area at the offset angle.

Chimney Materials

Many kinds of masonry, brick, concrete, concrete blocks, stone, or hollow clay tile are suitable for chimney walls. Following are recommended minimum thicknesses for wall sections:

Brick, lined, not less than thickness of standard brick, 3¾ inches; exterior walls exposed to very severe weather not less than 8 inches. Unlined, not less than 8 inches with inner course preferably of firebrick.

Hollow tile or concrete blocks, lined, and not less than 8 inches.

Stone, lined, and not less than 12 inches.

Concrete, lined, not less than 4 inches. Unlined, not less than 6 inches. Concrete chimneys require vertical and horizontal lacing of steel reinforcing rod.

Prefabricated Chimneys

Prefabricated or patent chimneys are good alternates to masonry chimneys and both are somewhat less expensive.

Prefabricated chimneys come in snap-together or twist lock sections made of two or more insulated metal cylinders separated by insulating material and/or air spaces.

Patent chimneys consist of round metal flues lined with terra cotta and protected on the outside by metal casings. Building codes require 1 to 2 inches of clearance between outer casing and woodwork. For further details and sketches, see the chapter on metal fireplaces.

Insulation

Leave a firestop space of 2 inches between all wood beams, joists, floors, and the outside face of chimney walls. Fill this space with loose crushed cinders, mortar refuse, gypsum block, or other noncombustible material. Solid mortar, concrete, or masonry is unsuited for this purpose.

If the chimney is at least 8 inches thick and lined, clearance between chimney and wood construction may be reduced to ½ inch. Authorities recommend adding a cement plaster coat to masonry chimneys that are to be encased by wood paneling or other combustible materials.

Set wall studs to insure 2-inch clearance between studs and chimney masonry. Plastering may be done directly on chimney wall or on raised metal lath laid over the masonry. Plastering directly on the wall is preferable because it will not crack when the chimney settles.

If the exposed upper section of the chimney is subject to severe winds, its walls should be at least 8 inches thick. If chimney walls are less, enlarge them, starting at least 8 inches from roof rafters or joist.

Height of Chimney

To prevent the upward draft from being neutralized by downward eddies from neighboring roofs, build your chimney flue at least 3 feet above flat roofs and 2 feet above the ridge of pitched roofs. At elevations above 2,000 feet, the height of the chimney should be raised slightly or the flue area should be increased. Rough rule of thumb is to increase both height and cross-sectional area of the flue about 5 percent for each 1,000 feet above sea level. Consult architect, local building inspectors, or masonry contractors for data.

Where roof conditions keep you from going the recommended height above the roof, a tile chimney pot may give the effect of the necessary additional height. Chimney hoods of metal, brick, stone, or tile also prevent back drafts. Place the hood with its closed sides against the direction of air currents. The open area of the hood should be at least four times the cross sectional area of the flue.

Spark Arresters

Spark arresting screens are an advisable safety measure, especially in a wooded area. They are required chimney components in some building codes. Use a rust-resistant wire mesh or perforated sheet metal with openings not smaller than ½ inch nor larger than ⅝ inch. The top of the screen should be at least 12 inches above the cap.

HOW TO ADD-ON
A MASONRY FIREPLACE

Adding on a fireplace is not a simple job, an operation that can be completed in one or two weekends—in fact, the clutter may be with you for a month or two. The wall and floor have to be opened and their internal framing rebuilt so they will not be weakened. Then there is the usual digging, mixing, and bricklaying that goes with any fireplace building job. Later, finishing handwork will be necessary to mend the broken plaster, restore the flooring, and fit the flashing around the chimney on the roof.

Many masons feel that fireplace building is an art, and no book of rules and equations will ever show *them* how to do their work. It is not surprising, therefore, that the number of ways to build a fireplace increases with the number of masons you talk to.

The drawings that follow show in a general way the steps usually followed in building a simple fireplace. They are not assembly instructions, nor do they attempt to cover all the variations that local building practices and ordinances tend to create.

The first step is to draw up plans and material lists. Refer to your house blueprints to determine if the dimensions of your fireplace will fit into existing framing and to make sure that you will not be cutting into plumbing, wiring, or furnace ducts. When your plans are complete, check them over with your building inspector and, if practical, with your architect.

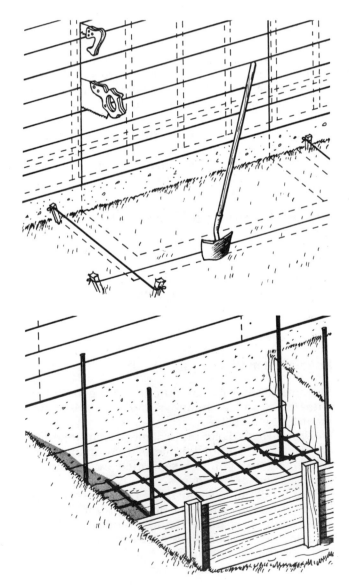

1. Laying Out the Job

When you have decided on the spot for building the fireplace, draw lines on the outside wall where you are going to cut. Be sure to avoid laying the line over a stud. You can tell where studs are by pounding on the wall with a hammer (the stud responds with a solid thud), by measuring from a nearby door or window (studs are usually set 16 inches on center), or by boring an exploratory hole or two. Then lay out the boundaries of your foundation pit with string. Since the foundation will have to be at least six inches larger all around than the chimney, allow yourself plenty of digging room. It will also be wise to crawl under the house to see what you are going to encounter when you open the floor.

2. Digging the Foundation Pit

Dig out the foundation pit to meet your boundary lines. Expose the concrete house foundation and dig down below and under it. The proper depth will depend upon local conditions—frost, soil type, building ordinances. Thoroughly clear off the concrete foundation. Build forms to hold the wet concrete foundation to the exact outside dimension of the slab. Place ½-inch reinforcing steel in grid form, 12 inches on centers, 5 inches from the bottom of the pit. For added strength, set four steel rods vertically so they will extend up into the *inside* corners of the rough brick firebox. Allow concrete to cure for a day or so. Keep covered with straw, dirt, sacking, and keep damp for a week or ten days.

3. Opening the Wall

The next step is to open the wall and expose the studs. First, bore a hole in each of the upper corners of the opening. Start cutting with a keyhole saw and transfer the job to a sturdy cross-cut that won't be ruined if it encounters some nails. Cut down to floor level and pry off the outside wall covering — siding, shingles, stucco board. Remove the protective waterproof paper beneath it, then take out the diagonal sheathing. Cut open the inside wall and remove the laths or plasterboard. Do not cut the studs—just clear out everything around them, including any cross-bracing. Better have a heavy tarpaulin near at hand to nail over the opening, for it will probably be gaping open for several days.

4. Cutting the Studs

Don't forget that the studs are holding up your roof, as well as keeping the wall in place. Before you cut them, therefore, make provision for carrying the load while the wall is open and temporarily weakened. One way is to transfer the load to a pair of 2 by 6s placed between floor and ceiling inside the room. To spread the load, butt ends to the uprights against 2 by 8 planks, one on the floor, one against the ceiling. Cut uprights about ¼ inch longer than the space measure and force them into position. When placing the ceiling cross-member, be sure it runs crosswise to ceiling joists. Or if joists run in same direction as the fireplace wall, place the cross-member so it rests under a joist rather than between two of them.

5. Opening the Floor

Before cutting into the floor, finish off the wall opening. Note how the finished opening is framed: the load formerly carried by the cut studs is dispersed along a pair of 2 by 6s, placed side by side over the top of the hole, and carried down to the sill along doubled studs on both sides. Doubled studding is also run up to the plate. Remember that once the floor joists are cut, the floor is weakened unless additional support is installed. Set a girder (6 by 6) under the joists *before they are cut.* Support it on posts resting on precast concrete piers. Leave girder and piers in place after the floor is finished. If you wish to avoid cutting the floor, plan for a cantilevered, elevated hearth—but first see your architect and building inspector.

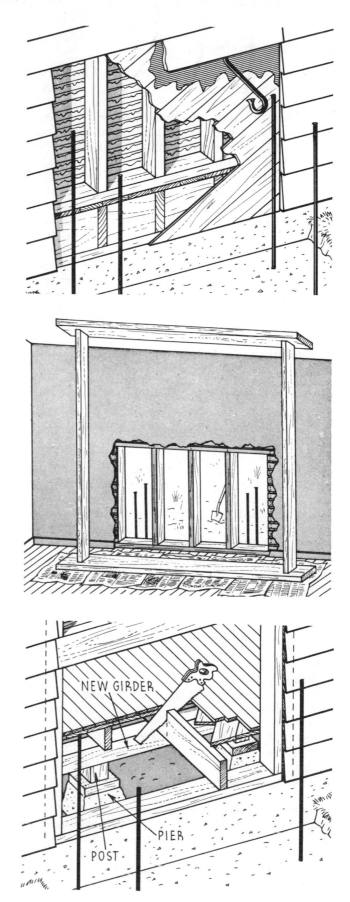

6. Finishing the Floor Opening

Finish off floor construction by rebuilding floor substructure so it can carry the load once borne by the joists you have cut. Save all material; you will need it later. First, measure and cut two lengths of timber to fit across the exposed ends of the cut joists and butt snugly against the uncut joists on both sides of opening. Nail firmly in place. As an optional step, support the ends of the cut joists in iron hangers as shown in the drawing. If subflooring is easy to get at, you may want to double the joists on both sides of the opening. They should be doubled back to the first girder. This may not be a simple task, especially in an old house, where wiring, plumbing, bridging, and natural floor sag will interfere with running new joists that far back.

7. Building the Ash Pit

You are now ready to start the brickwork. Clean all dirt off the top of the concrete foundation slab so the mortar will stick to the slab. Lay a wall two bricks wide across the front and back, one brick wide on the sides. Butt the front wall against the foundation. The two short walls, inside the box, do not have to be locked into the structure. They support the firebox brickwork. Use Type B mortar. The vertical reinforcing rods should be bedded in masonry to protect them from rusting out. Lay bricks across the corners and fill in with grout. Be sure to mortar the clean-out door securely into place so that hot embers will not escape.

8. Forming the Subhearth

With pit finished, you are now ready to start the subhearth. Keep a wary eye on dimensions to be sure that the surface of the finished hearth comes out flush with the finish flooring. Figure down from the floor surface. Allow for the finished hearth (¾ inch for tile, 2¼ inches for brick), a bed of mortar (at least ½ inch), and at least 6 inches of concrete subhearth. Total: 7½ to 8¾ inches. Wooden forms hold front hearth in place while concrete is setting; loose bricks, resting on ½-inch steel rods, support back hearth. Latter may also be supported on wood (remove through clean-out door after concrete sets), solid brickwork, or steel plates. Place a grid of reinforcing steel 3 inches below the top of the slab and pour in concrete.

TEMPORARY SUPPORTS

9. Finishing the Subhearth

The cut-away drawing shows the finished concrete slab in place. The slab, cantilevered out from the front wall of the ash pit, will be anchored under the weight of brickwork to be laid on the rear hearth. Any irregularities in surface—such as a low point above the brick roof—may be corrected with mortar when the finished hearth is laid. Note the placement of the reinforcing steel mat. Wooden forms that supported the front hearth are removed after the concrete has set. Vertical steel reinforcing rods are continued through slab to be cemented in brickwork around firebox.

10. Finishing the Hearth

Lay the finished hearth as soon as the hearth slab has set about 12 hours and the outer brickwork has been brought up a few courses. The inner hearth is laid with firebrick, bonded to the subhearth with fireclay-cement mortar. Note that the firebrick floor covers only the area needed for the firebox. When these bricks have been laid, they are usually covered with a layer of sand to protect them from mortar drops as the masonry grows. The front hearth—usually laid with tile or common brick—can be set at this time or postponed until the facing is laid in place. Note masonry ties, inserted in the mortar joints, for anchoring the facing when it is attached later.

11. Laying the Firebox

The firebrick walls of the firebox may be laid at the same time as the outer brickwork, or they may be held off until the outer work reaches damper height. Firebricks are usually laid in a cement-fireclay mortar, mixed to consistency of soft butter, and applied in a thin layer ⅛ to ¼ inch thick. Bricks are set on edge or laid flat. If laid flat, they give greater strength to the wall. Side walls are slanted inwards about 4 to 6 inches. The space between the side walls and the outer brickwork should be filled with broken bricks or other bits and pieces of masonry, slushed in loosely to allow for firewall expansion.

FILL WITH
BRICK SCRAP

24"-84"

20"-24"

30"-90"

20" min.

12" min.

12. Setting in the Back Wall

First lay the back wall plumb for about 12 inches, then slope it forward to reflect heat outward and to provide for a smoke shelf. The angle of slant depends on the size and height of the fireplace. Since side walls are usually laid to butt against it, they have to be cut at the back end to meet the angle of sloping wall. One way to cut side walls is to put top courses of brick in place dry, hold a straight board against the rear edge of the wall slanted at proper angle, and draw a line along edge. Then disassemble the upper wall, cut bricks on line, and mortar into place. After both side walls are laid, the back wall may be mortared in. The first course above the straight wall is tipped by making a wedge-shaped joint higher in back than in front.

13. Providing a Damper and Smoke Shelf

Except for smoke domes that both eliminate part of the masonry and have an incorporated damper, dampers fall into two main categories: blade and dome dampers. In the blade type, the damper door is hinged or swiveled in a flat frame. In the dome type (see drawing), the door is fitted into a metal housing shaped into a throat. Some dome dampers are designed with a front edge that serves as lintel for fireplace facing, but most of them simply support masonry of the inner brickwork. Dampers come with a choice of controls for opening and closing. Some controls extend through the facing, some work by chain, some are operated by a poker.

DOME
DAMPER

14. Finishing the Facing

Build up the firebox, place the damper in position, and build the facing. Don't forget to stop your masonry 2 inches below the wall cross-framing. And remember to wrap the ends of the damper in fibreglass wool. To obtain smooth mortar joints on the facing, use a mason's pointing trowel (better practice with it on some rough brickwork first). Restore the inner wall surface with patching plaster or strips of wallboard. Lay the hearth up to the wood flooring, then fill in the gap with strips of subflooring and cover with finished flooring, salvaged from that removed when you cut the floor.

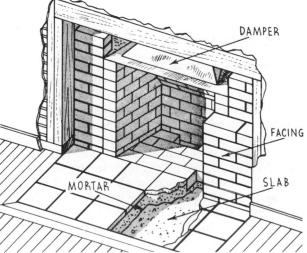

DAMPER

FACING

SLAB

MORTAR

15. Choosing A Prefabricated Fireplace

Instead of building the firebox, you can use a prefabricated fireplace that incorporates all the vital parts — firebox, damper, throat, smoke chamber, lintel, and flue collar. Installation of such a unit simplifies the task of building a fireplace, for the masonry is merely laid around it, and the unit insures proper and exact proportions of the critical parts. Metal units are manufactured in a choice of sizes and styles (the one in the drawing is a composite by several firms). Some are equipped with hot air circulating ducts that permit the fireplace to double as a hot air furnace. (See page 75.) They are usually built in, with a surrounding mat of fibreglass.

16. Using Weatherseal

To make certain that water will not seep into the house around the edges of the fireplace opening, seal all points where masonry passes through the woodwork. Around the sides, where masonry butts against doubled studs, bricks should be laid against waterproof paper and then caulked with a mastic compound. Across the top of the firebox, metal flashing is needed to divert water away from the opening. Slip one angle of the flashing under outer wall covering, cover with weatherproof paper, and then nail on the finished covering. The angle of the flashing that fits into the brickwork should be mortared into a running joint and sealed with mastic. Top flashing is shaped to overlap sides so that it will shed water at the corners.

17. Building the Throat and Chimney

Brickwork on both sides of the firebox should be stepped in for six or seven courses until the throat narrows down to flue size. Lay the last course to provide a slight ledge for the flue tile to rest upon. Smooth off the inner surface of stepped-in bricks to assist the passage of flue gases. Fill in with mortar or bevel bricks. Before setting the chimney, fasten weatherproof paper on the house wall where bricks will rest against it. Cement the tiles in place and lay the bricks around them. (If bricks are laid first, the new masonry is likely to be damaged when the heavy tiles are positioned.) To cut a tile, place a cement sack inside, fill tightly with sand, and sever with a series of cuts made with a chisel.

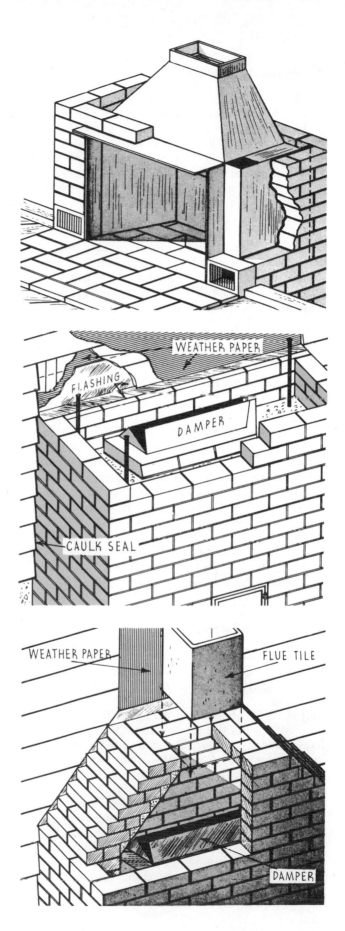

18. Penetrating the Roof

At the point where the chimney passes the roof line, it is necessary to cut into the roof in order to install an anchoring device to brace the chimney. Clear away the shingle or composition roof surfacing for an area a good foot larger all around than the opening needed for the chimney. Mark cutting lines on the roof sheathing 2 inches wider than each side of the masonry and saw out the pieces. Remove enough of the sheathing so you can freely reach the plate. Cut off the tips of the rafters, if they extend beyond the roof line, flush with the outside wall. If your house is equipped with gutters, cut them with a hacksaw. Note the reinforcing steel in each corner of chimney masonry, sealed in with grout.

19. Tying-in the Chimney

The chimney should be anchored to the house framing by some means. There are several ways to do this. In the drawing, a 1-inch iron strap is bent around a tile and the reinforcing steel, twisted to pass flat through a mortar joint and nailed to the plate or to a rafter. If the ceiling joists run parallel to the wall, fasten cross members to the joists. Repair cut gutters by filing off rough edges and soldering caps on each of the cut ends. Be sure to buy caps of the same metal as the gutters, otherwise electrolytic reaction between the different metals will corrode edges and destroy the seal. (Better be sure, too, that there is a downspout to drain each of severed gutters.)

20. Fitting the Flashing

Install metal (copper, lead, galvanized iron, aluminum) flashing around chimney to seal the opening against water leakage. Flashing is applied in two layers. The bottom layer (B and E in drawing) is fitted under the roof covering and bent to lay flat against the brickwork. The second layer (A, C, D in the drawing) is cemented and caulked into the masonry and fitted so it overlaps the first layer. This is known as cap flashing. Except where they overlap, flashing joints should all be soldered. Allow some leeway between cap and base flashing to permit the chimney to settle or move slightly without rupturing the seal. The flashing along the upside of the chimney (B in drawing) should be bent up in the center—a demanding job that should be done by a sheetmetal shop.

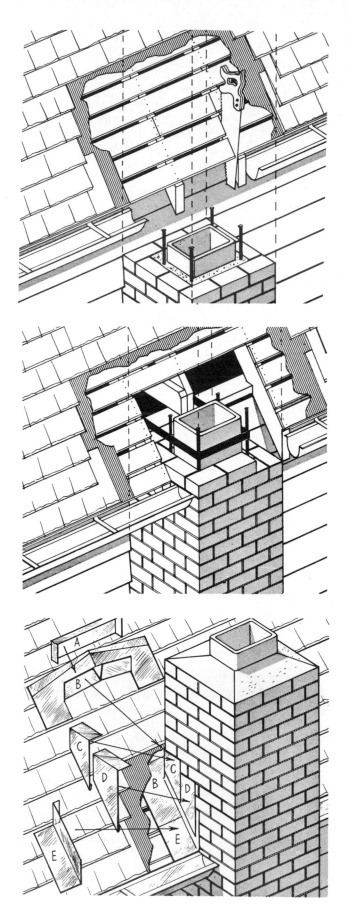

The prefabricated fireplace

Most building codes now approve a variety of prefabricated fireplaces. The job of installing one may be easier and far less expensive than you think, especially if you are remodeling. When the house is being built, a masonry fireplace is only slightly more expensive than installing a metal fireplace. Once your home is built, though, the cost of masonry rises to more than twice the price of a prefabricated fireplace. To add-on a masonry fireplace, you will have to lay a concrete foundation, walls must be ripped out, and a mortar mess kept under control, possibly for several weeks.

Beyond their low cost and ease of installation, the prefabs have other advantages. They're guaranteed to work, if properly installed. Their relative lightness (250 to 500 pounds) eliminates the need for special foundations; you can install one in an inside wall or on a second floor (special flues permit stacking fireplaces on several floors).

You can choose from many brands and hundreds of styles. Manufactured fireplaces fall into two categories—conventionally designed built-in units and contemporary freestanding models. On the next page, you'll find 18 popular styles.

Conventional Designs

Built-in units are usually positioned in or against a wall. Available in different sizes from 28 to 42 inches wide, these units can be disguised to look like a masonry fireplace by facing them with brick, stone, tile, marble, or some other traditional noncombustible material.

Snap-together flue sections eliminate special tools, and simplified instructions help to make installation possible for the average homeowner. Some metal fireplaces come equipped to receive gas lines for gas logs or log starters.

Most built-in packages have multiwall construction so they require no insulation and can actually touch combustible house walls. Because of the "zero clearance" feature, once the surround (the mantel and the side pieces) and the hearth are installed to meet code requirements, the rest of the unit can be faced with almost any material.

Heat Circulating Fireplaces

How can you be sure that your fireplace will heat a room completely without the discomfort of varying temperatures and possible smoke? Special built-in fireplaces known as heat-circulators are designed to act as sources of heat for large areas. When burning, they draw in cold air, warm it, and emit the heated air through vents. This can be very desirable for cabins or any place where a supplementary heat source is desired. These,

One of three built-in prefabricated fireplaces in rambling hillside home located in Woodside, California. Architect: Goodwin Steinberg.

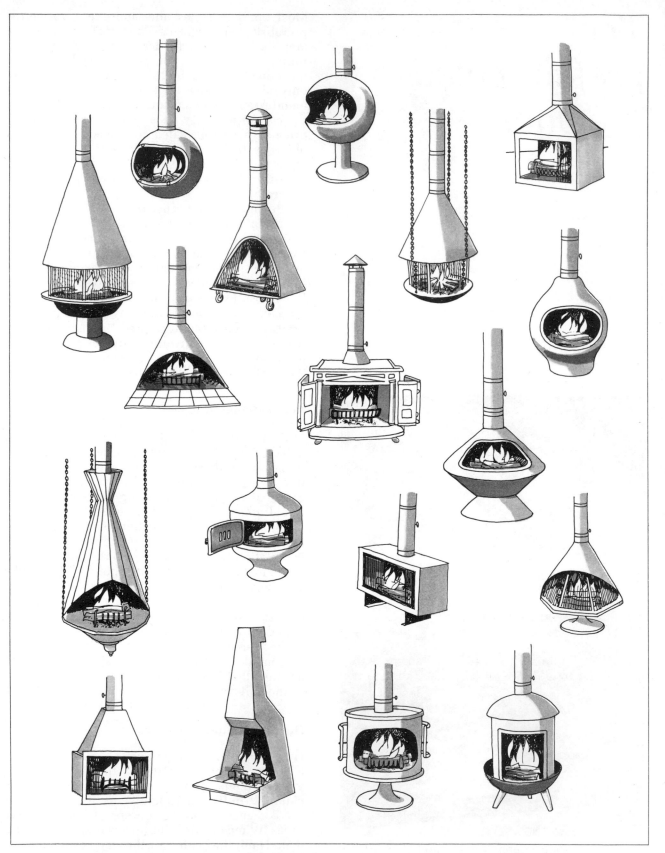

Fireplace variety *is available in today's marketplace. Here are only a few of the hundreds of styles being offered by fireplace manufacturers. Prices range from under $500 to around $1,500.*

also, are guaranteed not to smoke. *Caution:* Be sure that the heat outlets are not located opposite your central furnace thermostat.

The heat-circulator is designed to circulate heat through a room. It does this by heating air in strategically located metal ducts and returning the warmed air to the room. The air ducts can be extended into other rooms so that the fireplace can distribute heat to rooms at the sides or in back of it, or upstairs. In operation, heat circulating units overcome several deficiencies of the standard fireplace. All fireplaces, of course, require air for draft with oxygen for combustion. This action sometimes causes uncomfortable temperature variations, since the air at floor level, drawn toward the fire, is colder than air at shoulder height. In standard fireplaces, after the air has warmed, most of it disappears up the chimney. The heat circulator puts the warm air to work heating the room. It draws cool air to inlets placed at low levels, heats the air, and releases it through outlets placed where desired.

To further improve circulation, an electric ventilating fan can be placed in the pipe, either at the cool air inlet or heated air outlet. Manufacturers specify fans that suit their units, and some make grilles with the fan built in.

Tests show that these units have distributed warm air to corners of the room that were cold when a noncirculating fireplace was in use. Temperatures of over 200 degrees have been recorded at outlets. This increased heating efficiency does not mean circulating units can replace central heating furnaces in colder regions, but it does demonstrate that where a fireplace is the only source of heat (as in a cabin), heat circulators do an effective job.

Location of inlets. The air intakes may be located to draw in fresh air, or they may be placed inside the house, where they draw on indoor air at room temperature. In some localities, the indoor inlet is efficient because in extremely cold weather, the frosty outdoor air may not become sufficiently warmed before being emitted into the room.

Indoor inlets. When the inlets are installed indoors, they are placed at floor level to draw in the cool air that settles to the floor.

Inlets may be exposed on the front or side of the fireplace facing, their openings covered with metal, brick, or stone grilles. Those with thin, closely spaced horizontal fins are pleasing in appearance. If exposed grilles and openings displease you, raise and extend the hearth to cover them.

If the fireplace is in the end wall of a very long narrow room a ventilating fan will increase the heating action of the fireplace. Locate cool air inlets in the opposite end wall. Install fans in these to speed the flow of cold air toward the fireplace. Connect the inlet with the fireplace by an inlet pipe. The fireplace manufacturer will give you full specifications. You can also do this with a fireplace located in the side wall.

Fresh air inlets improve fireplace drafts and prevent smoking.

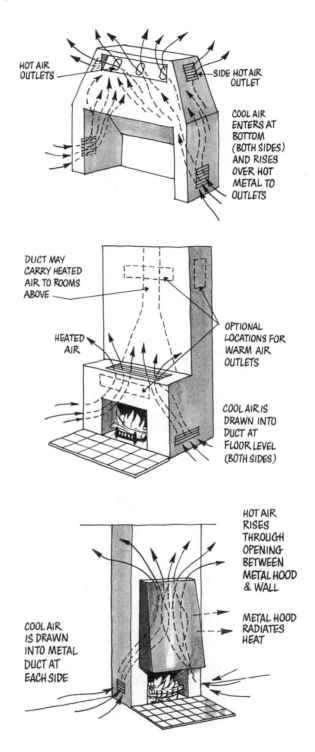

Fireplaces may draw a volume of air equal to two or three large roomfuls through the chimney at frequent intervals. Thus, in tightly constructed, efficiently weatherstripped houses, enough replacement of air cannot be drawn indoors to supply the chimney draft. A partial vacuum results, pulling smoke back into the room.

A fresh air circulator draws outdoor air through a grille in the outside wall of the fireplace or through a pipe connected with an outside wall vent.

Location of outlets. You can place heated-air outlets anywhere it is convenient. The front or side faces of the fireplace are the usual locations. Outlets may be placed directly over the fireplace opening, in the top of the mantel, or in the front or sides of the chimney wall close to the ceiling.

If you can't locate the outlet anywhere except in the front wall above the fireplace opening, you can conceal it with a light decorative shield of the same material as the walls.

A combination of outlets is practical. An outlet close to the ceiling on each side of the fireplace will distribute heated air to its own section of the room. Design variations: air circulating units may be installed in conjunction with a metal hood, which hides a front outlet. Special forms are built for see-through and projecting corner fireplaces.

Heating other rooms. Heat circulators can supply warm air to rooms behind the fireplace if ducts and outlets are provided.

Heated air can also be supplied to rooms back of or at the side of a corner fireplace. A standard circulating unit with rear inlet openings designed for corner installation is available. You can heat upper rooms from the circulating fireplace. Use a supplementary ventilating fan if you wish to be sure this unit will spread heat uniformly. Of course, any change from the manufacturer's standard position of inlets and outlets requires additional expense for fireproof piping.

Contemporary Freestanding Fireplaces

Modern freestanding fireplaces are generally less expensive and easier to install than built-in units because the only installation cuts required are through the ceiling and roof. Most of them also require non-combustible floor covering and heat shields on walls near the fire.

Available in an endless variety of colors and shapes, they offer a few advantages over built-in models. Their hoods and stacks can help to heat

a room rapidly, making them ideal for cabins. Their minimum silhouettes allow you to position them in front of windows so that seating can be arranged to focus on a view as well as on a cozy fire. Seating then allows more people to enjoy the fire simultaneously.

Not all prefabricated fireplaces meet code requirements in all areas, so check with your local building officials before buying one. Since any kind of fireplace is considered a permanent addition, a building permit is required before installation.

Prefabricated Chimneys

Unless the fireplace hooks into an existing flue, you will have to install a chimney. You buy the prefabricated chimney as a part of the total fireplace package. The chimney comes in snap-together sections, usually consisting of an inner insulated steel pipe and outer pipes separated by air spaces and more insulation. Many of these are triply insulated, the air spaces between the pipes working so efficiently that the outside pipe is cool to your touch.

A patent chimney is required by building codes in some areas. This is a terra cotta flue liner surrounded by an incombustible metal casing. The casing may be left exposed, sheathed in another decorative metal sleeve, or concealed inside the walls of the structure. If you install a metal stack inside a wall, you will probably have to maintain

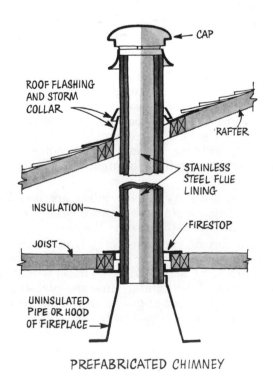

PREFABRICATED CHIMNEY

a minimum distance for combustibles and ventilate the collar that joins the stack to the wall.

You can obtain a patent chimney from a sheet metal contractor. It is not likely that you will find one in a fireplace shop.

Gas-fired and Electric Fireplaces

In the days when homes were constructed without fireplaces, attempts to simulate the hearth were frequently a source of amusement. Some were dangerous and building codes ruled against them.

Today, engineered units with convincingly realistic designs make it possible for mobile homes, apartments and homes in woodless areas to include a decorative simulated hearth. A versatile range of BTU ratings enable the gas-fire and electric fireplaces to heat almost any size room or dwelling.

If you own a cabin and prefer to do other things with your weekends than cutting and splitting firewood, you may be interested in the gas-fired models that are equipped with outlets for extensions to other rooms. Some of them can generate enough heat to drive you out of the room.

Simulated fireplaces are complete units. When you move one into your home and connect it to your gas line or plug the electric model into an outlet, it is ready to heat the room. For the gas-fired fireplace you may have to run a line to its location. Some of the units are fitted for optional thermostat controls which function in the same manner as a gas furnace or wall heater.

Installation of the electric models is simplicity itself. If you can hang a painting, you can install one of these.

HOW TO INSTALL
A PREFABRICATED FIREPLACE

"Official approval" is the key phrase to remember when you're installing a prefabricated fireplace and chimney. You must obtain a building permit.

Most building inspection departments now routinely approve installation of any fireplace and chimney that has passed the rigorous tests for UL (Underwriters' Laboratories) or ICBO (International Conference of Building Officials) approval. Fireplaces and/or chimneys not having UL listing or ICBO approval must meet the complex requirements of the Uniform Building Code, which is interpreted differently in various jurisdictions.

Chimneys are required to extend at least 3 feet above the highest point where they pass through the roof of a building and at least 2 feet higher than any part of a building within 10 feet. Try to choose a place for the chimney so that joists, trusses, or rafters will not have to be cut where the chimney passes through the ceiling and roof.

The step-by-step sequence on the next page is a general guide compiled from several sets of manufacturers' instructions. Your particular fireplace will have individual engineering features that require more detailed information. Building codes specify that the manufacturers' instructions are to be followed precisely.

Prefabricated heat circulator *unit fits safely against combustible floor or wall. Warm air outlets may be directed toward front or ducted to other rooms.*

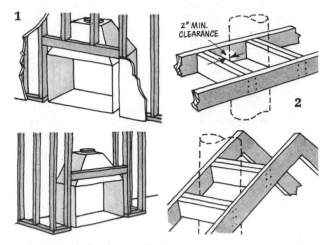

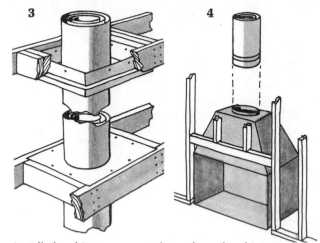

1. Position the fireplace in the location you have selected. Here are two methods of framing the unit. You will find that the chimney installation is easier if you frame-in after the chimney is installed. **2.** Cut and frame the opening for the chimney in your ceiling and roof, allowing a 2-inch minimum clearance from combustible materials. It is a good idea to use doubled headers, as shown, for the framing. **3.** In a one-story house,

install the chimney support box where the chimney passes through the ceiling into the attic. In a two story house, install a firestop at the first ceiling level and a support box at attic level. **4.** Insert the starter chimney section into the top of the fireplace. Follow the manufacturer's instructions for locking it into place. Here you may need someone to hold the starter section while you lock it into place.

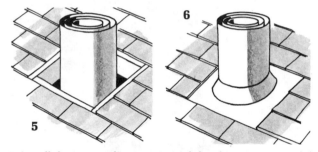

5. Install the intermediate sections of the chimney as you did the starter pipe. Continue with these until the top section extends through the roof. It should rise high enough to allow the flashing to be fitted over it. **6.** Fit the flashing over the chimney pipe and nail securely to the roof frame or rafters. Use nails with a neoprene washer or cover nail heads with a waterproof mastic. Do not nail the lower flange. **7.** Finish

roofing around the chimney. Cover the side and upper flange of the flashing with roofing material but cover the roofing material with the lower part of the flange. See illustration. **8.** Lock the final chimney sections into place to the desired height. Place the storm collar down over the pipe until it touches the flashing. Seal the joint between the pipe and storm collar with a waterproof mastic.

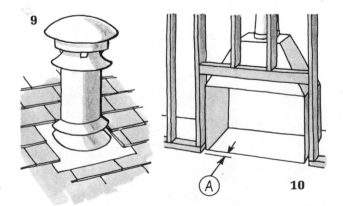

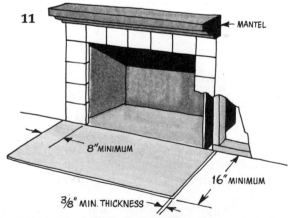

9. Attach the adaptor and/or chimney cap. Open chimneys do not stain as readily as those with caps, but they do not keep rain out. In wooded areas you may also need a spark arrester to keep sparks in and birds out. **10.** Frame the fireplace with 2 by 4s as shown in step number 1. If, as shown here, the finished facing is to be flush with wall A, allow space for facing between the wall surface and the fireplace. **11.** Cover

the framework around the fireplace with any desired wall material—sheetrock, plaster, paneling. Now install the finished facing directly to the steel face of the fireplace with a suitable adhesive. The hearth extension must be a non-combustible material extending minimum of 16 inches in front of the fireplace opening and 8 inches on each side. It must be 3/8-inch thick. Use a suitable adhesive for installation.

The firetender's manual

How to tell if firewood is seasoned; how to buy the wood; precautions when storing firewood; woods that burn fastest and slowest; how to color the flames □ useful and decorative accessories for the fireside □ how to solve a smoke problem □ how to build a fire. □ devices to improve heating efficiency.

Buying and storing the wood

Ideally, firewood should have been cut during the preceding winter or spring and seasoned through the summer and fall. If it is not seasoned, it won't burn well. Firewood is still green if it looks freshly cut or shows moisture when struck with a hammer.

WOOD TO BURN

A standard cord of firewood has logs 4 feet long stacked 4 feet high and 8 feet across. This measures 128 cubic feet. Firewood is also sold by the half cord, by weight, bundle and truckload. Prices vary in each area. A few phone calls to dealers listed in the yellow pages under Firewood will tell you what the going rate is for a cord, half cord or truckload. There may be a delivery and stacking charge added to the price unless you pick up the wood yourself.

Every firetender has his own favorite woods. For a rip-snorting crackling blaze with plenty of sparks flying, softwoods are favored. Popular softwoods are pine, poplar, fir, and elm. Softwoods, however, if used consistently, will leave soot deposits on flue walls.

For a much longer burning fire and one that is quieter, use such hardwoods as oak, hickory, madrone, manzanita, maple and eucalyptus. The heat given off by either softwood or hardwood is about the same. Hardwoods, though, leave less residue and will not excessively coat the flue with soot.

Charcoal and Wood Substitutes

Some firetenders prefer charcoal or a mixture of charcoal and wood. Charcoal gives off an impressive amount of heat—twice that of wood. It heats by direct radiation, and once started, it burns long and steadily. Charcoal briquets often give off more heat than the raw form and burn without sparking. Charcoal is favored for barbecuing in the fireplace. *Caution:* because of the danger of being overcome by carbon monoxide (which cannot be detected by the senses), always provide ample ventilation when burning charcoal in an enclosed area.

Logs of compressed sawdust offer an effective, if relatively expensive, fuel. They burn with greater heat than wood, giving off 75 per cent of the heat of coal.

Aroma and color. Many woods burn with a pleasing aroma and color. Dried pieces of pine blaze with enthusiasm and a woodsy odor. Eucalyptus is pungent; even a handful of pods from the tree produces a fragrant odor.

For colorful flame, no fuel can match driftwood for its blue and lavender fire. Aged pieces of applewood also burn with rainbow colors and an appealing fragrance.

Flame Colors from Chemicals

Colorful fire may also be produced by chemical means. Copper chloride produces strong blue and green flames but will also yield some purple, pink, and yellow fire. Copper chloride in technical crystals is preferable to the chemically pure form. If mixed with other chemicals, it should be blended in a glass container, for it deposits copper plating on any metal that it touches.

For a strong red flame, use strontium chloride. If it is not obtainable, try strontium nitrate. It may be mixed with copper chloride to add to the rainbow effect. Chemically treated composition logs that burn colorfully for two or three hours are available in nearly every supermarket. As firewood prices go, these are fairly expensive.

Common table salt (sodium chloride) gives off a brilliant yellow fire. It tends to cancel out other colors, so use it sparingly in combinations. If you wish to mix these three chemicals, blend 2 parts copper chloride with 1 part each of strontium chloride and table salt. Chemicals may be tossed directly on the fire, or they may be mixed with water and soaked into the fuel ahead of time. Pine cones and charcoal should be immersed in the solution for several hours.

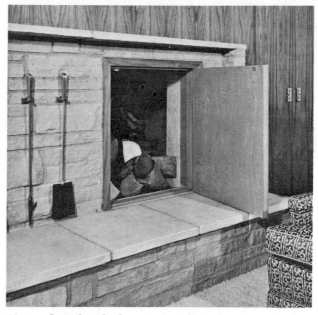

Now you see it, *now you don't. The door of this wall hatch for wood storage is covered to blend with wall.*

Firetender's log locker *in handiest location. Locker door matches wood paneling above fireplace.*

Hearth sofa *is composed of bleached clay tiles, padded with vinyl covered foam rubber cushions and soft throw pillows. Wood storage between fireplace and entrance at left is architectural feature.*

STORE THE WOOD NEARBY

A hungry fireplace can consume several armloads of fuel in the course of a long evening. A busy firetender comes to appreciate the convenience of having ample wood nearby so he doesn't have to carry it in from the garage or struggle with it up the basement stairs any more often than necessary.

There are practical ways to provide for fuel storage in a fireplace plan. The most convenient arrangement is a fireside locker with a door that opens outside or into the garage. This permits the wood supply to be stacked in place without tramping winter mud or snow through the house or leaving a trail of bark, pitch, splinters, or a dropped log here and there. Inside the room, the wood cabinet itself can easily be integrated with the fireplace and wall design. The door can be balanced with other living room cabinets or concealed in wood paneling.

Sometimes, it is desirable frankly to expose the pile of wood, stacked in a recess or under a cantilevered hearth, to display the promise of long, enjoyable fires.

Be a little cautious about where you keep the main wood supply. Termites love firewood, but they avoid the sun, so it's a good idea to find someplace outdoors for the woodpile if possible. Stack the wood on a bed of crushed stone so that it won't come into contact with the soil where the bottom logs will rot. If you must stack the wood indoors, try to keep it out of contact with wood doors, floors and walls.

Accessories for the fireside

Railing around hearth, *called a fender, was used to prop feet, dry socks. This one, along with andirons and firestarter, is primarily for decoration.*

Accessories—the tools of the firetender—add a finished look to the fireside. Usually included in a fireside setting are a log grate or set of andirons, a brush, poker and shovel set, a firewood holder and a bellows. Matched ensembles are available for a formal appearance, or you can shop around for the individual tools you want. The variety is almost limitless.

When you consider fireplace accessories, keep in mind the ways you may entertain at your fireside. In addition to the usual fireplace tools, a fireplace shop will have useful and decorative fireplace cooking accessories, containers for keeping food warm or hot, plus cranes, hooks, spits, stationary or pivoting grills.

Because the fireplace has been around since the days of our cave dwelling ancestors, it has acquired a share of strange artifacts. One of these, very practical in its day, was the *curfew* (or fire cover). The curfew is a good example of what you can turn up if you enjoy hunting for fireplace curios.

In the 9th Century, the Normans had a strictly enforced law that required covering all fires at the sound of an evening bell. The word curfew means, quite literally, firecover. The instrument employed for compliance with the Norman law took its name from the bell.

Curfews are still in use in some parts of England, where it is claimed they have kept the same fires burning for over 100 years.

Wrought iron and brass *ember guard and brass coal scuttle add touch of elegance to ordinary fireplace. Coal scuttle here is used to hold logs and kindling.*

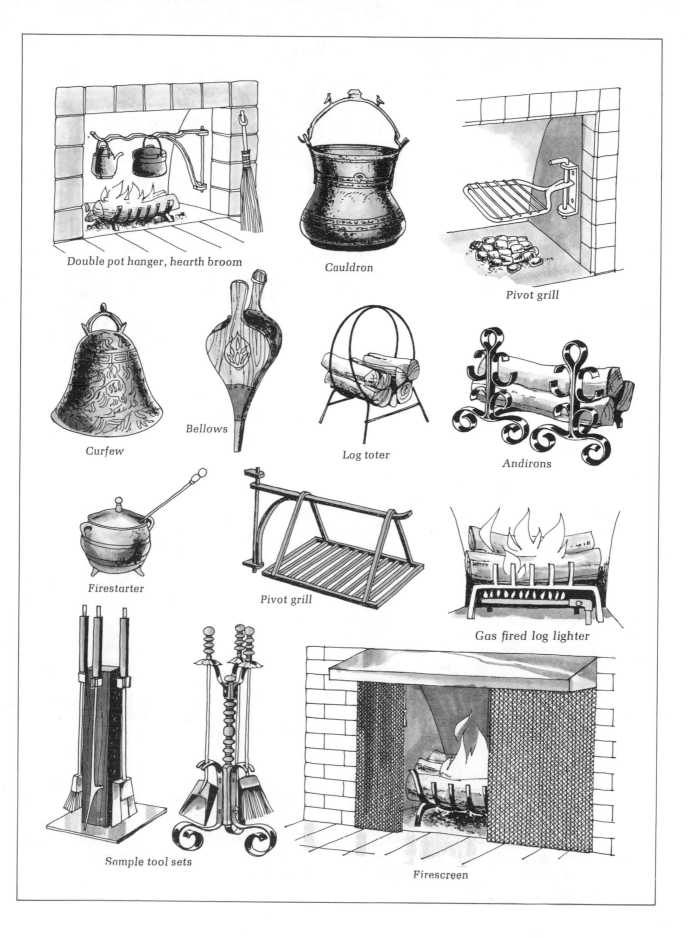

Double pot hanger, hearth broom

Cauldron

Pivot grill

Curfew

Bellows

Log toter

Andirons

Firestarter

Pivot grill

Gas fired log lighter

Sample tool sets

Firescreen

Heat recovery devices

Here's how they work: *Arrows show how heat is directed into the room by these four basic devices, either by convection or radiation.*

Though a crackling blaze in the fireplace does much to warm the soul, surprisingly little of the fire's heat actually contributes to warming the room. In fact, in the conventional masonry fireplace, close to 90 percent of the fire's heat is lost up the chimney.

Heat recovery devices, as their name implies, recover some of this heat and direct it into the room where it's needed. The devices covered here are easily adapted to existing masonry fireplaces at a cost that is modest to moderate. Most are simple in design and function, requiring no special tools or skills to install. You can recapture additional heat by using two or three of these devices in combination or by buying a system that integrates them into a single unit. (See facing page.) To find suppliers of this equipment, look in the Yellow Pages of the telephone directory under "Fireplaces."

Types of Devices

Heat recovery devices take advantage of the ways heat travels: *radiation* (direct transmission of heat waves or infrared rays) and *convection* (warm air currents set up by rising heat).

Optimum radiation grate. Resembling an ordinary fireplace grate, this device directs more radiant heat into the room by exposing more of the log's burning surface and embers to the front of the fireplace.

Tempered glass screen. Convective currents from a fire burning in an ordinary fireplace can actually pull warm air from the room up the chimney. Also, the unrestricted flow of air into the fireplace causes the fire to burn too fast, consuming large amounts of fuel. A tempered glass screen with a controllable air intake allows you to regulate the burning rate so less heated room air is sucked up the chimney and fuel is conserved by slower burning.

Convection grate. This device consists of a series of C-shaped tubes fastened to a metal framework. When the tubes are heated, rising convective currents inside pull cool air into the bottom openings in the tubes and expel heated air through the top openings. Similar devices use fans to circulate air through the tubes, thereby increasing efficiency.

Metal heat reflector. This metal sheet is positioned behind the fire to reflect, into the room, heat normally absorbed by the back wall of the fireplace.

Combining devices. An optimum radiation grate and a tempered glass screen are a good combination to increase radiant heat. You can also buy devices that combine the glass screen with a convection grate—with or without a circulating fan. With a little ingenuity you can even contrive your own heat recovery system, using devices on the market or inventing them yourself. When shopping for heat recovery devices, make sure you have the dimensions of your fireplace handy so you can assure a proper fit.

Combination unit *employs convection grate, glass screen, and fan; fits most fireplace openings.*

Modification *of the standard convection grate uses a fan to force air through the tubes; principle is similar to that of a forced-air furnace.*

Tempered glass screen *is more than attractive—it allows you to control the fire's burning rate. Closing the doors keeps sparks and embers inside.*

Healthy fireplaces don't smoke

Fireplaces smoke for a number of reasons. The worst offender is the downdraft. Not only will it make your fireplace smoke, but it can also cause your furnace to operate erratically. The solution may be as simple as opening a window slightly somewhere in the room or in another part of the house.

Modern homes are sometimes so tightly built that they don't admit enough air to feed a fireplace. And when the furnace is operating, its draft may draw air out of a tight house, creating a partial vacuum and pulling air (and smoke) down the chimney to replace it. Installing an adjustable vent in the foundation wall usually solves this problem permanently.

Outside Drafts

Nearby tall trees or the slope of hills close to your house can send air currents down the chimney. Even the slant of one's own roof will often angle unwanted drafts into the flue. The flue should be built at least 3 feet above a flat roof and 2 feet above the ridge of a pitched roof. The top of the chimney must be 2 feet above any point of the roof within 10 feet of the chimney. If your chimney height meets these minimum standards and downdrafts are still a problem, you may need a chimney cap.

You will find two basic types of caps: the stationary cap and rotating cap. A rotating cap always faces away from the wind (because it has

a rudder on top, it cures many stubbornly smoking fireplaces). Stationary caps are more attractive, however, and if the downdraft problem has been correctly diagnosed, they do an effective job.

Where a fireplace is located opposite an outside door, gusts of wind may cause an uneven flow of air whenever the door is opened. Smoke is then pushed into the room. Conversely, smoke is often pulled from the fireplace by an exhaust fan operating in the kitchen. To solve the gust-of-wind problem, either place a fairly solid room divider between the fireplace and the outside door or install a draft inducer (a fan that draws hot air up and out the flue). There will be a rather substantial heat loss but no smoking. The kitchen fan difficulty is solved more simply—turn fan off.

Especially in a vacation cabin, birds and small animals left undisturbed for weeks or months at a time have the chance to build nests in the flue. You can check this by lowering a light on an extension cord into the chimney from the roof.

If there is no obstruction, the trouble could be an improperly built fireplace. Remedying that could require the services of your neighborhood masonry expert. Before you call in the mason, though, check the construction ratio tables on page 65 against the dimensions of your fireplace. You may find that your fireplace opening is too large for the flue area. You can decrease the opening by building up a brick hearth or the front border of the fireplace. Easier, and perhaps the best solution, is to obtain a firebox insert from a fireplace distributor. Look in the yellow pages under Fireplaces. These are prefabricated steel additions that you simply slip into your present fireplace and surround (front side only) with a border of noncombustible material. Check your local building code for minimum clearance.

For structural defects such as off-center flues, sharp angle in the flue passage, projection of pipes into flues, or double use of single flue, call for professional help.

Removing Smoke Stains

Smoke stains on fireplace masonry can be removed with a solution of one-half pound of tri-sodium-phosphate dissolved in a gallon of water. Apply with a scrub brush but wear rubber gloves. The solution may irritate the skin. Muriatic acid (a parlor name for hydrochloric acid) will often do the job, but it may discolor the brickwork. Never use it on stonework. Because muriatic acid is a powerful chemical, it should be treated with respect. Mix 1 part acid to 10 parts water in a wide-mouthed jar, pouring the water in first, then adding the acid. Apply with a cloth and rinse with water immediately.

How to build a fire

Building a fire in a fireplace looks easy enough. Almost any kind of shavings, wood chips, logs or debris will burn. All you need is a large supply of matches and extraordinary patience. But, there are simpler ways to attain a steady, even-burning blaze. This review of the fundamentals may help to ensure consistent success for your fire-building technique.

Laying a Good Fire

First open the damper (if you keep it closed when the fireplace is not in use, to prevent heat loss from the house). The fire should be laid on andirons or a fire grate. Lacking these use a pair of small green logs so that air will reach the fire from below. The ash level should be about an inch beneath the andirons—for a good fire it is not desirable to remove all of the ashes.

Here is one of several good ways to lay the fire:

Put several sheets of crumpled or twisted newspaper in the center of the fireplace, then crisscross several sticks of kindling on top of the paper. Kindling should be any fast-burning wood, split to about one or two-fingers width. Place three fairly small logs over the kindling, one on top of the other two, split sides down. It is a mistake to expect bark to ignite faster than the split surface. Bark is nature's effective insulating material against heat and other elements.

The three logs confine the heat to the heart of the fireplace, each radiating heat to the other. But don't stack them so tightly that the fire can't escape upward and burn freely.

Just before you light the fire, you can start a good draft up the chimney by lighting a crumpled sheet of newspaper placed on top of the logs. Or, hold the newspaper high in the throat. If the fireplace has been idle for an entire season, place the newspaper above the damper and set it afire. This takes the chill from the chimney and helps get the draft started. Then you can light the paper beneath the kindling.

If your fireplace lets smoke into the room, open a window so the fire can draw more air to sustain an updraft. (See *Healthy Fireplaces Don't Smoke.*)

Many people lay the fire in different patterns according to their needs. A large log, placed near the back of the fireplace with smaller logs burning in front of it will radiate more heat into the room. If the room tends to overheat, build a smaller fire behind a large log placed near the front of the andirons.

The screen should remain closed unless you closely watch the fire and are burning a hardwood that won't throw sparks. Don't burn wrapping paper during the holiday season; flames from gift-wrappings can become surprisingly large very quickly and scraps of burning paper might be carried to the roof by the updraft. Repeated use of your fireplace as an incinerator will fill the flue and smoke shelf with soot.

If you go to bed before the fire has burned down, stand the remaining logs in the back corners of the fireplace. They will usually go out quickly and be usable for the next fire.

Wood-burning stoves

The wood burners available today are a mixture of old and new. Most units are easy to install and offer a rustic charm you can't get with modern heating devices. Large or small, simple or ornate, there's a wood-burning stove to fit any room in the house where heat is needed.

Pot-belly stove

Kitchen range

Parlor stove

Box stoves

Scandinavian stoves

Yukon (barrel) stove

Cook stove

Wood-burning stoves come in many sizes, shapes, and designs. The ones shown here are the classics; their designs have stood the test of time.

Practical heating with a touch of nostalgia

Around the turn of the century, the once-prevalent wood-burning stove was all but abandoned in favor of more efficient fossil-fueled heaters. In recent years, though, the venerable "wood burners" have been making a comeback. Today, you'll find a wide variety of these stoves on the market—from authentic reproductions of the pot-belly stove and the cooking range, to modern thermostatically-controlled wood-burning heaters designed to fit contemporary decor.

Where wood is readily available, many people find wood-burning stoves and heaters a practical solution to the rising costs of conventional heat. Others simply enjoy the nostalgic charm of firing up a grand old parlor stove or cooking on a wood-burning range.

The Basic Kinds

Some stoves, like the box stove and the pot-belly stove, are named for their appearance. Others are described by the location they heat, such as parlor or kitchen stoves. Many times they're simply defined as heating or cooking stoves and referred to by brand name. The stoves illustrated on page 91 are the classics.

How They Work

Unlike fireplaces, wood-burning stoves work on the principle of controlled combustion. By regulating the airflow into the stove, you control the burning rate and hence the heat output. Modern "airtight" stoves are sealed tight except for one or two adjustable air inlets or dampers that direct air precisely where it's needed for efficient combustion. These dampers are either manually operated or controlled by a thermostat. Properly loaded, many airtight stoves will hold a fire up to 12 hours without reloading. They may also be left unattended during this time without danger of sparks or embers flying out into the room.

Most older stoves and older stove designs are not airtight. The amount of air flowing into these stoves through unintentional as well as intentional openings is usually controlled by a damper located in the stovepipe.

CHOOSING THE RIGHT STOVE

Before you buy any stove, consult your local building department. There are two good reasons to do this—in most communities, the stove and its installation must pass a building inspection; in addition, your building inspector can help you plan a safe stove installation. You can also get advice on installing stoves from a reputable stove dealer. For more tips on safe stove installations, see page 95.

In order to choose the right stove for your heating needs, you should seek advice from people with experience in heating with wood. Local stove dealers are a good source. When shopping for stoves, take along a rough floor plan of the area you'll be heating. The plan should indicate room sizes, number and sizes of doors and windows, and where the stove will go.

Cozy addition *to a bedroom or small den, this tiny pot-belly stove helps provide a feeling of intimacy, is ideal heater where space is limited.*

How Well They Heat

Most wood-burning stoves are designed to heat one or two rooms only. If you're planning to use the stove to supplement your existing heating system or to heat a room addition or small cabin, you'll have to match the stove's heat output to the space you'll be heating. If you decide to heat your entire house with wood, you may need several stoves, along with some type of fan or vent system to carry heat into outlying rooms. Or you may want to install a wood-burning furnace, some of which are equipped to burn coal, fuel oil, or natural gas also.

Most stoves are rated according to the number of cubic feet of living space they'll heat. The figures by themselves do little more than tell you that one stove will throw out more heat than another. The amount of room space a stove will actually heat depends on a number of factors, including local climate, position of the stove, amount of insulation and weatherstripping in the house, and the number of openings in the room.

Fuel Efficiency

Though the amount of heat a stove produces is important, the amount of wood required to produce that heat is equally important—even more so if wood is expensive in your area. A stove's fuel efficiency is the percentage of wood's potential (stored) heat the stove converts into useful heat (that heat which contributes to heating the living space). These percentages often appear in the literature provided by the stove manufacturer. If a stove is 60 percent efficient, it will produce twice as much heat with the same amount of wood as a stove that is only 30 percent efficient, all other things being equal.

Look for Quality

Durability and ease of operation are two traits common to quality stoves. Some stoves built during the Victorian era are still in service today—testimony to the fact that a well-built stove will last a lifetime if properly cared for. Good stove designs, too, stand the test of time.

Stove construction. As with other appliances, the quality of workmanship and materials that go into a wood-burning stove is important. Today, stoves are made of cast iron, plate steel, or a combination of the two.

Cast iron stoves are made from separately cast plates, which are bolted together and their joints sealed with furnace cement to make them airtight. Eventually the cement will become brittle and fall

Screened door *on this ornate parlor stove lets you view the fire. Chrome hood pivots out to expose small cooking surface. (See back cover.)*

out, and it must be replaced when it does. Cast iron is extremely hard and has a tendency to crack if the plates are cast too thin or the stove gets too hot.

The durability of a plate steel stove depends on the thickness of the steel and the quality of the welds that hold it together. If the steel is too thin the stove may warp under extreme temperatures. A slight warp usually won't affect the performance of the stove, though it won't do much for the stove's looks. More serious warping may break the welds, causing the stove to lose its airtightness.

Both materials are susceptible to corrosion from repeated firings. Of course, the thicker the material, the longer the stove will last. Many stoves have replaceable metal or firebrick linings that help protect them from warping, cracking, and corrosion.

Whether you're buying a new stove or an antique, check it carefully. Even new cast iron stoves may have cracks due to improper casting or damage during shipping. On steel stoves, check all welds carefully for bubbles or cracks that may cause air leaks. On all stoves, make sure the loading door is properly aligned and seals tight against the stove body.

Some of the antiques you'll find may have tiny cracks; they can be repaired—patched with furnace cement. If the cracks are large, the stove is virtually useless. Most old stoves will show some signs of corrosion inside the firebox. However, if the firebox walls are less than 1/16 inch thick, the old trooper is nearing the end of the trail.

Ease of Operation

If you're planning to use your stove often, you'll appreciate one that's easy to use and requires little attention. The chores of refueling the stove and removing the ashes can become tedious, so before you buy a stove, find out how often these chores must be done. Some stoves have the convenience of an ash removal pan to make unloading neat and easy. Otherwise you'll need a small ash shovel or ash rake and a metal ash bucket.

Also, some stoves are easier to load than others. A large loading door is a plus—it allows larger pieces of wood to be burned and reduces the chances of getting burned on the stove while loading. If the door is located near the bottom of the stove, there's less chance of smoke puffing into the room when you're feeding the fire, though you may have to get on your knees to load the wood unless the stove is placed on a raised hearth.

Quality stoves usually have insulated door handles. With other models, you'll have to keep a heavy glove handy once the stove gets hot.

Stove Accessories

There are a number of devices on the market designed to increase the heat output of wood-burning stoves. Called heat extractors or heat exchangers, these devices are usually attached to the stovepipe to recapture warm air that would ordinarily be lost up the chimney. If you intend to buy one of these devices, check with your stove dealer to make sure the device you choose is compatible with your stove installation.

You'll also find ones for heating water. Some, like the heat exchangers, attach to the stovepipe; others are designed to fit inside or attach to the stove. Another device, popular with woodburning connoisseurs, is the flue oven shown above.

You'll find a variety of items available to aid in stove operation and maintenance. These include ash buckets and shovels, pokers, prongs, and bellows for tending the fire, and stove polish for cast iron stoves. However, devices or items that are absolutely essential to the stove's operation or installation—such as stovepipe, fire-proofing materials, grates, and dampers—are not considered accessories and should be figured into the initial cost of the stove.

Flue oven *fits standard stovepipe, complements barrel-type design of stove beneath. Damper below oven controls cooking temperature.*

Homemade pies *seem to taste better when baked in a wood-burning range. This one's an antique; similar versions are still being manufactured today.*

Modern *wood-burning heater has thermostatically-controlled damper, heat-circulating fan.*

SAFE INSTALLATION AND OPERATION

Through their dependence on wood, our grandparents gained a healthy respect for fire and the damage it could do. The possibility of a stove-caused fire can be reduced to a minimum if you install the stove properly and use it safely.

Installing Your Stove

These are the three prime ingredients of a safe stove installation:

Adequate clearance. Stove and stovepipe must be kept a safe distance from all combustible materials and surfaces.

Proper insulation. Stovepipes must be insulated where they pass through walls, ceilings, and roof.

Wall and floor protection. Combustible walls and floors near the stove must be covered with a non-combustible material such as asbestos board or masonry.

Combustible walls or floors are defined as those containing wood, whether or not they're covered with a combustible material. To protect these surfaces, you can use masonry (brick, stone, ceramic tile) or a combination of sheet metal and asbestos board. The recommended thicknesses and installation of these materials will vary slightly according to local building codes. The drawing at right shows the minimum allowable clearances for the stove and stovepipe as set forth by the National Fire Protection Association. They're meant to be general guidelines only and may differ from clearances prescribed by the stove manufacturer or local building codes.

Using Your Stove

Always follow the stove manufacturer's recommendations for safe stove operation. It's usually possible to burn a hotter fire in the stove than is recommended, but this is bad practice—if you continually over-fire the stove you will decrease its life and increase the possibility of fire.

Inspect the stovepipe occasionally to make sure all connections are tight. If you're continually burning small fires in the stove or using softwoods for fuel (see page 82), excess soot and creosote will build up in the stovepipe. Creosote, a flammable substance formed by tars and acids in the smoke, is the cause of chimney fires. If you use the stove regularly, you should dismantle and check the stovepipe at least twice a year for creosote buildup. There are chemical cleaners available for removing creosote from the stovepipe.

The stove itself should be checked now and then to make sure it is working properly. Some stove doors have asbestos gaskets that must be replaced occasionally. The damper in the stovepipe should also be working properly.

When using the stove, it's always a good idea to have a fire extinguisher handy. If the fire gets too hot, you can control it by throwing several handfuls of baking soda on it. Never dowse the fire with water, because the sudden change in temperature may crack or warp the stove.

Always keep combustible materials (newspapers, furniture, wood, for example) away from the stove.

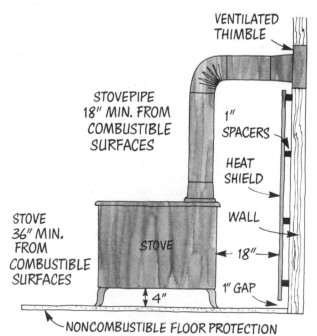

Photographers

Jerry A. Anson: 31. **William Aplin:** 35 top, 37, 39 bottom. **Architectural Photographers:** 39 top. **Morley Baer:** 33 bottom. **Chapin Bowen:** 41 bottom. **Jerry Bragstad:** 56 bottom right. **Ernest Braun:** 2, 3, 17 top, 19 right, 20, 23 top left and right, 24 bottom, 27 bottom, 36 top, 40, 50 bottom. **Clyde Childress:** 29 bottom, 42 top. **Glenn Christiansen:** 25 right, 26 top right, 27 top right, 46 top, 51, 55 right. **David Cornwell:** 26 bottom right. **Robert Dawson:** 53 bottom four. **P. A. Dearborn:** 47. **Dearborn-Massar:** 21 bottom left, 49 top right, 83 top right, 83 bottom left. **Walter Diblee:** 12 bottom. **Philip Fein:** 36 bottom, 46 bottom. **Richard Fish:** 18 bottom left, 45, 60 bottom, 83 top left. **Gerald R. Frederick:** 4. **Frank L. Gaynor:** 16/17 bottom, 18 top, 33 top left. **Heatilator Company:** 12 top, 29 top, 79. **Art Hupy:** 32. **Frank Jensen:** 42 bottom, 55 left. **Edmund Y. Lee:** 34 left. **Ellsworth Marugg:** 22/23 bottom, 75, 84, 93, back cover. **Philip L. Molten:** 28 left, 63 left. **Tad Nichols:** 33 top right. **Don Normark:** 19 left, 21 top, 28 bottom right, 41 top, 48 bottom, 60 top, 87 bottom right, 92, 94 bottom. **Maynard L. Parker:** 5, 16 top, 18 bottom right, 35 bottom, 44, 49 bottom left. **Ron Partridge:** 57 top. **Chas. R. Pearson:** 49 bottom right. **Photographic Reproductions:** 25 left. **Norman A. Plate:** 52 left, 87 bottom left, 95. **Karl H. Reik:** 22 top, 30 top, 64. **John Robinson:** 26 bottom left. **Martha Rosman:** 21 bottom right, 27 top left, 57 right. **Julius Shulman:** 24 top, 56 bottom left. **Douglas M. Simmonds:** 49 top left. **Hugh N. Stratford:** 54. **Thermograte Enterprises, Inc.:** 87 top. **United States Stove Works:** 30 bottom. **Darrow Watt:** 11 bottom, 62, 89. **R. Wenkam:** 34 right, 48 top, 59. **Mason Weymouth:** 57 bottom left. **Peter O. Whiteley:** 94 top. **W. P. Woodcock:** 52 right, 53 top.